Wit, Wisdom, Insight & Expertise

by

Members of
National Speakers Association –
Austin Chapter

Debbie Pearson	Helene Segura	Cheryl Jones
Kent Cummins	Jack Allen	Lisa Walker
Lee Mocyzgemba	Patricia Selmo	Patti DeNucci
Dave Swanson	Sharon Schweitzer	Jim Comer
Donn LeVie, Jr	Mickey Addison	Carrie Vanston
Teri Hill	Mardi Wareham	Paul O. Radde, Ph.D.
Scott Carley	Jill Raff	Nancy Hopper
Floyd McLendon, Jr		Mike Robertson

The art of writing is the art of discovering what you believe.

— Gustave Flaubert

Table of Contents

Healthcare Hurdles............................ Debbie Pearson 1

Discover the Magic!.............................. Kent Cummins 8

The Divine Download .... Lee Mocyzgemba 16

Resilient Leadership .... Dave Swanson 23

Get More Gigs! ....Donn LeVie, Jr 32

What's the Next Conversation?.................. Teri Hill 41

Fractured Teams from Broken Trust .... Scott Carley 49

Hard Earned Lessons...........................Floyd McLendon, Jr...............................57

Control Your Brain, Enjoy Your Life ..... Helene Segura 64

Confidence ....Jack Allen..72

From Ideas to Action .... Patricia Selmo 80

A Question of Culture.......................... Sharon Schweitzer 87

The Five Be's for Entrepreneurs............ Mickey Addison 93

The Gorilla Says Yes! ....Mardi Wareham....................................99

Transforming Transactions Into Interactions™ ....Jill Raff 106

Don't Take Anything Personally...............Cheryl Jones.. 114

Success Over Obstacles............................Lisa Walker 121

Quality Over Quantity...........................Patti DeNucci.......................................128

How to Survive Caregiving .... Jim Comer 136

Crucial Keys to a Thriving Business Culture ....Carrie Vanston....................................144

You Must Be Present to Win .... Paul O. Radde, Ph.D. 153

Who's Behind the Curtain for You? ...... Nancy Hopper 161

CardBored.......................................Mike Robertson 168

Notes from the Editors

What a privilege I had, being the first to read each of these 23 chapters by my friends and colleagues at NSA Austin!

Some came with almost no editing required. I read them and sent them along to Mike with the challenge, "Find the typos...I can't!" Others arrived in a variety of different formats, requiring some work to make them fit comfortably into the format of what I have been calling, "The Book." But each chapter is worth your time, to read and get to know this diverse group of remarkably talented and caring people.

I read, re-read, and edited more than 65,000 words in less than two weeks. (I write a column for a magic magazine which is 2,000 words each month. So this was like editing nearly three years worth of columns!)

I had to remind myself that it was just one book. I can read a book in less than two weeks... especially such a fascinating collection of life stories and ideas. No two chapters are the same, but the one thing that you will get from all of them is the reminder that we create our own reality... and that we have the power to make that reality FANTASTIC!

– Kent Cummins

I am grateful to Paul Jenkins, a member of the Mountain West chapter of the National Speakers Association, for the inspiration for this book. At the NSA Winter Conference in February 2017, Paul showed me the book their chapter had published, featuring seventeen of their professional members. I instantly loved the idea and, when I returned to Austin, I shared it with the director of our chapter's writers group, Kent Cummins. He was equally enthused and you hold the result in your hands.

In this volume, you'll be able to sample the talent and passions of 23 wonderful speakers from the Austin chapter, and you're certain to find at least a handful of topics that will be both interesting and helpful. From memoir to business guidance, from caregiving to networking, NSA-Austin has an expert who can enliven your next conference or meeting. Please enjoy the thoughts and wisdom of my friends; many have included contact information if you need to learn more. Thank you for reading!

– Mike Robertson

Healthcare Hurdles

by Debbie Pearson

It will happen to all of us.

By the time most land in the trenches of healthcare, we find ourselves in a tornado of terminology beyond our comprehension and circling the moat of medical morass with no clarity. Emotions run rampant and we find ourselves being sucked into the vortex common to victims.

This is true if the crisis arises for yourself or someone you love. Our medical system offers an abundance of barriers, piles of paperwork, and confusion at a time when all we want is some sort of certainty. And the truth is, life offers no guarantees.

After more than forty years as a nurse, I have found there are no simple answers. Only stories to be told. Tales that paint pictures to illuminate the path ahead; a road to walk with greater confidence and control. The only truth I know for certain: hope is not a plan.

MEDICAL MIRACLE?

Donny was one of my patients with a plan for the majority of his life...but not for everything. A man who squeezed every drop from life. Drinking deeply from all aspects — family, faith, work, and play. While raising children, the family lived in 5 countries — allowing his kids to touch the texture of the world — experiences that can't be taught, only lived. And they lived it fully.

Once their three children were educated and out of the nest, Donny and Gail (his wife), were ready for the "couple time" that had been eclipsed by decades of responsibility. First was the dilemma of where to settle. With no misgivings, they moved to New York City! This was *their* moment. They had everything they needed: time, resources, and health...for a while.

Then Donny noticed changes in himself — a disturbing disconnect between his brain and his legs. It was as though the wiring was severed. Even laser focus on movement was fruitless. His legs were like lead. Something was very wrong.

Time for action! Rounds with specialists. Blood work. Scans. Physical therapy. The works. Not what Donny & Gail had planned for at this stage, but the elusive answer was priority #1.

Their answer was devastating. A rare form of Parkinson's Disease — one that projected a life expectancy of perhaps a year, if all went well. Suddenly the sharp focus on fun morphed. It was a time for reality and establishing a plan for their finite future together.

Donny & Gail got their affairs in order and relocated from New York to Austin where family lived. They moved into a single-story home that was handicapped accessible. And they made a solemn vow — to live each day with a single focus: quality of life.

Every day was delicious — a beautiful sunset, rain that made the air smell sweet, Blue Bell ice cream (before the Listeria). The time left would be cherished, the memories a treasure.

Three months elapsed without a hitch. With a fierce focus on safety, falls were minimized. Their new life plan was calm and gratifying. But Donny did have a cough he couldn't shake. It started as simply annoying but progressed to the point of disturbing his sleep. After one fitful night of coughing, Donny was visibly ill, running a fever, and short of breath. EMS responded quickly — off to the hospital. Upon arrival in the ER, things looked grim. The fever was high, blood pressure alarmingly low, and Donny was unresponsive.

The culprit was pneumonia that had traveled to the bloodstream. Donny was in septic shock, not expected to survive the illness. Gail went crazy. She wasn't ready. They had only had three of the twelve months promised. As tears flowed, the begging increased. The doctor simply had to do something. Anything! She needed more time to prepare herself.

Out of compassion, the doctor admitted Donny to the hospital and started IV antibiotics. Day 1 — no change. Day 2 — a ray of hope: the fever was inching down and blood pressure was creeping up. However, Donny remained unresponsive. He couldn't get out of bed, walk, talk, eat or drink. His body was there but not the rest of him.

Gail grabbed that glimmer of hope and ran with it. She knew what Donny was capable of. All she needed was to buy time. Get him home where he could recover and return to her. The doctor threw her a lifeline — a permanent feeding tube. She signed the consent before she even asked what it meant. Because what it meant to her was what she wanted most — time.

They went home with the feeding tube — inserted directly into his stomach — where Gail learned how to administer liquids, medications, and nutrition. This would buy her the needed months. Surely he'd recognize family and respond.

Can anyone guess the ending? Seven years in a persistent vegetative state with no end in sight. No indication of enjoyment. No communication. Only drain — of physical stamina, of emotions, of resources, and of hope. This is a true story, not a fairy tale. And nobody lived happily ever after.

The Truth About Medical Miracles

Medical miracles abound: artificial nutrition, pacemakers, respiratory support, organ transplant, dialysis, and so much more. The plethora of life support options available today will only grow tomorrow. But with every option, there is a price to pay. As insurance coverage shrinks, individuals bear increasingly more of the financial burden. Clarifying wishes in advance can be the kindest legacy you provide your family. A legacy that can span decades.

I believe that our ultimate healthcare entitlement is to choose for ourselves — what we want and what we don't want. However, opting in or out requires time, soul searching, and understanding options. Emotional decisions can have unintended consequences, for ourselves and our loved ones.

Advance planning is where kindness flourishes. A documented strategy saves family from standing at our bedside fighting over who can best read our mind. Each of us holds the power to bestow this treasure by following a structured blueprint of options. Serenity comes from choices that are both documented and communicated. That is where guilt evaporates and loved ones can bathe in the comfort of simply honoring wishes of the individual.

Making Decisions for Another

Surprisingly, the first step in making decisions for another person is to put your own opinions on the shelf. Neither your experience nor your opinions are required. Decisions based on *best interest* are not to be considered as the first line of decision making for another. Instead, *Substituted Judgment* is utilized as the highest ethical standard. Written into the Code of Ethics for the National Guardianship Association, this revelation is an eye-opener to audiences.

The basic premise is to make decisions by looking not through your own eyes but through the eyes of another person. To see not necessarily what is best medically, but what the other person would desire. Undeniably, this is formidable. The doctrine of substituted judgment asks a surrogate decision-maker to attempt to objectively determine, with as much accuracy as possible, what decision a now-incompetent person would make in a particular situation if he or she were competent to do so. This involves examining the individual's morals, beliefs and historical behavior patterns from the time he or she was competent.

Time after time, this doctrine has illuminated the darkness in presenting to audiences. When truly understood, they embrace a perspective that assists them in tackling difficult family situations. It's the stories that embed the lessons.

GUARDIANSHIP — WHAT DOES IT MEAN?

Gary suffered a massive stroke at the age of sixty-three, leaving him unable to speak, walk, feed himself or handle basic physical care. An unmarried loner, he'd left no clarity regarding his wishes and nobody in place to make his legal decisions. The medical system moved Gary through acute care and extended rehab for nine months. Although this is unusual, it sometimes happens. Only when options needed to be considered regarding discharge from rehab, was a brick wall encountered. Decisions needed to be made and there was no responsible party.

Gary's improvement over the nine months had been physical: walking, eating, and drinking. Sadly, he had not progressed in talking and reasoning. He was totally incapacitated, unable to return to independent living, could not name a responsible party, and needed court-appointed oversight. Nurses Case Management (my company) became his legal guardian.

The guardian role was to make choices for Gary as he would for himself if he could, following the doctrine of substituted judgment. But, what did Gary see, what did he want? His words were little to no help so observation of his behavior was the primary guide. His violent temper tantrums clearly indicated what he did not want and observation gave some insight in to his pleasures: TV, coffee, and smoking *frequently*. He also made it abundantly clear that he never wanted to be hospitalized again for any reason. The months he had spent in the hospital and rehab were akin to imprisonment in his mind. An agreement to support his wishes was made.

Our first step was to transition Gary to an assisted living facility for him to have his own apartment. His almost insurmountable challenge was to figure out how to smoke which could not be done in his room. Although it took weeks to learn, Gary eventually understood that his cigarettes and lighter were kept at the nurse's office. To smoke, he needed to pick up these items and take them outside to the designated smoking area. Afterward, they were to be returned to the same area. The fact that he eventually figured out this process was considered an overwhelming success.

Then one day Gary was found lying in his bed and unresponsive. Assisted living was no longer an option. The promise to not hospitalize him loomed large. What nursing facility would admit a patient in the midst of a medical crisis? Even more, what facility would allow Gary unlimited coffee and cigarettes? The possibility that he would recover spontaneously had to be considered as part of the plan. In today's society of non-smoking facilities and non-smoking campuses, smoking was a huge challenge.

Persistence was needed to convince the nursing facility that substituted judgment surpassed best interest...that his ability to smoke was a legitimate and appropriate goal. We had a solemn obligation to advocate on behalf of Gary's priorities. It took special negotiation and signed waivers of liability, but eventually we found a facility for Gary that allowed him to smoke at will in a designated outside area. Over time, he did recover and the temper tantrums subsided once he located his smoking bench. The doctrine of substituted judgment allowed him to set his priorities and guide his path.

Stories imprint where academic lessons fail. Tales allow the listener to touch the texture of lives that have lived the reality.

The Truth About Healthcare

Most of healthcare is not really healthcare. It's *sick care*. And a significant portion of sick care can carry pain: needles, tubes, tests, surgery, etc. But, there is a gentle option available in the cycle of care. Its name is hospice; a kind and comforting alternative to consider when the time is right. When you or your loved ones no longer want hospitalization and aggressive care, then it's time to seek a hospice consultation.

The biggest misconception is that hospice is only for the final stages at the very end of life. Patients benefit from this alternative far earlier than most think. A clear picture of hospice advantages might help sway the view.

Compassion Beyond Expectations

My mother, Louise, was one of those individuals who refused to plan. This went along with her belief that three things were not to be discussed: age, weight, and death. Therefore, as her Alzheimer's disease progressed, my father (Hymie) and I made decisions together for her using the doctrine of substituted judgment. For the large decisions, we were aligned. But many of the small day-to-day decisions, Hymie applied his own unique form of caregiving.

The day he decided it made sense to shave her hair like a military man, I had to step in. Knowing my beautiful mother, I knew she would be appalled. We started weekly spa days where I had the pleasure of doing her shower, hair style, full body lotion, manicure, and pedicure. This went on for years, even when Louise no longer knew my name. I knew who she was and that was all that mattered. These days always felt like a close, mother-daughter connection. At the end of one of our SPA days, my sweet mother took my face in her two freshly manicured hands, looked me in the eyes, and asked "Does your mother know where you are?"

For seven years, Hymie cared for Louise, at home, 24/7. She was always calm and happy, as long as she was in her familiar environment and cared for by family. Other people and other locations threw her into a tailspin of agitation. As she declined, lost weight, could no longer walk or talk, we decided she would not be able to tolerate the shock of hospitalization. She was admitted to home hospice care for the last two years of her life. Hospice provided the assurance that she would remain in her own cocoon of comfort at home with all care being focused on comfort and quality of life.

Home is where she died, peacefully in her own bed. Even though it was the middle of the night, the hospice nurse came out, called the physician, and they pronounced death over the phone. Then the funeral home arrived for transport. This is the ideal that most of us want. Even so, Hymie was devastated as his 24/7 job, his reason for living, was gone. Mercifully, time heals. Especially when surrounded by a large loving family. And by staying busy. Hymie focused on filling every moment with people, attending funerals, visiting nursing homes, doing story time every day at the preschool, volunteering at the Alzheimer's day out group, and traveling. His little red book stayed in his shirt pocket, always a full calendar.

Once he drove from Texas to Alaska — alone, in his little old car, with crank windows, a gym bag with a change of clothes, and a cell phone for emergencies that he never turned on. He was living the life of a bachelor. No wife or children to tie him down. He was back to being that quirky guy, loved by everyone who knew him.

And he watched his friends decline. He watched them die. But Hymie was different. He was still in control of himself at 91: walking like a young man, driving his own car, mowing the yard, edging it with a pair of scissors, living in his own home. Life was exactly as he wanted — a life where his domain was his own. So, he chose to end his life while still in control of himself.

A knife to the chest would have hurt me less.

But, even in death, the quirkiness remained. His suicide note began with loving words of good-bye and ended with an assignment. He had been trying to schedule his suicide for a while but life was too busy. He'd ordered a set of drums for the Alzheimer's day out group that he volunteered at every week. But there was a delay in the drums arriving. He had given my phone number to the music store to call when they arrived. Would I pick up the drums and deliver them to the group? When I did, a gloriously happy photo of Hymie was given to me that I'll forever cherish.

Because this was not an expected death and no hospice was involved, I'd like you to picture the parade of people who arrived at the scene: fire department, EMS, police, homicide investigator, crime scene unit taping off the entire house with yellow tape, coroner, and grief counselor.

Is that what you would want for yourself or any of your loved ones? Because they don't just show up to have tea. The questions they are required to ask inflict pain. It's like pouring acid on an open wound. And all the people who came for my father's death were not required just because of a suicide. These are protocols that must be followed for a death outside the hospital when the patient is not on hospice. They arrive to investigate and rule out foul play, regardless of age or circumstances.

In contrast, when my mother died, there was no parade of interrogators. Only the hospice nurse who came to calmly pronounce death and stay nearby for support. Does the magnitude of the contrast surprise you? If so, are you willing to consider hospice? Save yourself and your loved ones the additional trauma that nobody deserves, layered on top of raw grief.

Healthcare is only one of the four pillars of planning: legal, medical, financial, and personal. Any of the four parts can become an insurmountable hurdle for you or those you love. In contrast, when a clear blueprint is designed, you can pave a clear path for others to follow on your behalf. Gather your information, document your wishes, and avoid the unthinkable.

Debbie Pearson has spent decades caring for others, as a hospital nurse, a home health care nurse, case manager and court appointed guardian. She founded Nurses Case Management in 2000 to advocate for people who could no longer care for themselves due to age, injury or illness. Her two-book series (Age Your Way and the Blueprint to Age Your Way) guide patients and families through the myriad of decisions that often come out of nowhere when faced with aging, illness, or injury. As an experienced realist with a heart, Debbie inspires her audiences to face what is frightening and grab control from the morass of medical mazes. The magic is that the lessons learned are effectively applied to either the individual or family members. Debbie lives in Austin with her husband, Hank. They have three children and eight grandchildren.

Discover the Magic
How to live happily ever after

by Kent Cummins

I've been a magician for more than sixty-five years, but you don't have to be a magician to have a magical life. I'm writing this less than two months before my 75th birthday, and as I reflect on the many magical moments during those years, only a few of them involve actual magic tricks.

Building a puppet theatre in the garage during 6th grade was amazing. Designing and building miniature golf courses was magical. Playing piano in a rock and roll band in college was quite a trick! Juggling live hand grenades in Vietnam during the Tet offensive was unbelievable. Creating a chain of sandwich shops in Austin, Texas, was spectacular! And starting a summer camp for kids in 1993 may have been one of the most magical times of my life.

But the real magic has come from the people along the way. I have been blessed with so many interesting and caring friends, as well as a loving and supportive family. As I say in my juggling act while juggling three rubber chickens, "You may as well applaud now...it doesn't get any better than this!"

IT WAS A MAGICAL FAMILY.

My Grampa gave me my first magic trick. My Dad gave me the magic set that started me on the road to becoming a magician. My Mom made my first puppets, and became a puppeteer herself. My brother Carter designed and built many of my magic tricks. My sister Judy was one of my first beautiful assistants.

And then my life changed forever when I met Margot Lynn Grandjean in the seventh grade at Baton Rouge Junior High School. Ten years later, after we graduated from LSU, we got married. Two and a half wonderful kids (I'll explain in just a bit.) and two wonderful grand-daughters later, we are still having a magical life together.

Our 50th (golden) wedding anniversary was a Big Deal for us, because neither her parents nor mine had been able to reach that celebration before a spouse passed away. But when our 52nd anniversary approached, Margot asked me, "What is the 52nd anniversary?" I said, "Playing cards!" She laughed and said, "No, it isn't!"

But it was...at least for us. With the help of our daughter Carolyn, I put together a special deck of playing cards, with a picture from each of our years together on each card, and our wedding photo on the back. Take a card, any card!

THE AVERAGE AMERICAN FAMILY: 2 ½ KIDS!

But what about those "Two and a half wonderful kids?"

Well, after I got back from Vietnam, Margot and I put our lives—and our marriage—back together and had our first child, a son: Kevin Christopher Radley Cummins. Starting with my grandfather, Frank Carter Radley Cummins, every male member of our family had the "Radley" extra middle name. We were told that it used to be a hyphenated surname when he still lived in England. My full name is Kent Carter Radley Cummins.

My parents had three kids, Margot's parents had two, and each of us thought that our family was just right. So we wanted another child, but we really wanted it to be a girl...and couldn't figure out how to make sure that would happen. My sister Judy had four kids, all girls, and we didn't want to have that large a family. We also wanted them to be close together in age, and Kevin was already two years old.

It remained a conundrum, until I got Army orders to Korea...a country with too many orphans, most of them girls. While in Korea, we visited the baby home in Seoul and instantly fell in love with the first little girl that was presented as available. "You take her home now!" the attendant said. But we needed time to make sure this was really what we wanted...and it was.

We named our daughter Carolyn Kim Cummins. Kim is a popular first name in America, and the most common last name in Korea. It seemed to fit. Our little family was complete.

But then along came Brad Falch.

Brad was a friend of Kevin's from school, and his mother had cancer...and decided to go to Greece for an unorthodox cancer treatment. She asked us if we could take care of Brad until she returned after being cured. Margot and I talked about it, and then we had a family meeting including Kevin and Carolyn. We recognized that Brad's mom might not actually return, and we had to be prepared to take care of him until he graduated from high school.. The four of us agreed that we could do this.

Brad became our third child, but only for a few years. So we had one birth child, one adopted child, and one temporary, unofficial foster child. Two and a half kids: the perfect American family.

"Mysto the Magician!"

My life as a magician started on December 25, 1949, in my home town of Del Rio, Texas. I would be seven years old in just two weeks, but I was still in my pajamas when I walked out of my bedroom on the second floor and looked down at the huge Christmas tree, impossibly surrounded by more presents than I had ever seen before. There were toys, games, clothes, food... even an electric train. Christmas magic, to be sure!

When it was time to open my last present, it seemed the right size and shape to be another gamer, like Monopoly or Parcheesi...but we already had those. I ripped off the colorful paper, and couldn't believe my eyes. It was an A.C. Gilbert Mysto Magic Set! I didn't even lift off the top in front of my family. I carried it up to my room, closed the door, and only then opened the lid to this treasure chest of wonders.

I looked at all of the incredible things inside, and said, "I'm going to be a magician!"

Grampa (Mom's dad) was manager of the Buckhorn, a famous museum in downtown San Antonio, and he had given me a little magic coin box trick from their gift shop during the summer. Dad noticed how much I liked it, which inspired him to give me the magic set. Little did he know that this set would start a passion which remains to this day. I called myself, "Mysto the Magician," in honor of that set, not realizing that dozens (if not hundreds) of other little boys across the country were doing the same thing.

Mysto's first public show was in 1952, at my dad's dance recital, "The Cummins Colossal Circus." He made a place for me in front of the curtain while they were changing scenery, and I performed two tricks. I suppose he played music while I performed, because I know that I didn't talk. But at the age of nine, I was a magician!

The next year, my Uncle Vernon (The Reverend Vernon Carter Radley Cummins) booked me to perform my first paid gig, a show for the Junior Modern Woodmen Club in San Antonio. But I was still so shy that my dad did the talking for me. I got $3.00, which I spent at the Fun 'n Magic Shop in San Antonio. Now I was a *professional* magician!

No, really. Several years later, when I tried out for the Ted Mack Amateur Hour television show, they asked me if I had ever been paid to perform. I proudly told them about the $3 payment. "Then you're not an amateur!" they explained. I was not permitted to be on the show.

MY BEST FRIEND IS ALSO A MAGICIAN.

By the time I was at Baton Rouge Junior High School (yes, where I met my future wife), I was obsessed with magic. One day, I saw a boy walking down the hall with a magic book. I stopped him, and asked what he was doing with the book! He explained that he was a magician. "Oh, then that's okay." His name was John Schexnaydre.

John had suffered from Polio when he was younger, so I was a big fan of the March of Dimes, which helped to fight polio. One day, I went to the principal and said that I would like to do a magic show for the entire school, for the benefit of the March of Dimes. "We don't have room in the auditorium to let the whole school in for a show," he explained.

"Then we will need to do TWO shows!" Amazingly, he agreed. There are two interesting stories that I remember from those shows. The first was a performance of "The Razor Blade Trick," consisting of putting five razor blades into my mouth along with a piece of thread, apparently swallowing them, and then bringing them back out, neatly tied to the thread. (I know, perfect for middle school kids!)

To prove that the razor blades are sharp (They really were!), I sliced a piece of paper with each blade. On one of the slices, I accidentally sliced my finger, which started to bleed. I grabbed a handkerchief from my pocket, wrapped up the cut, and continued with the show. The next day, one of my friends said, "I liked your magic show, but pretending to cut your finger was pretty lame!"

The other memory was when I performed "The Watch Bag," a trick in which I borrowed a wristwatch from the Assistant Principal, put it into a red velvet bag (that Mom made for me), and proceeded to smash it with a balsa wood sledge hammer! At the end of the trick, the watch is produced from a nest of plastic eggs, without showing any signs of the savage beating. Or at least, that is the way I envisioned it.

But when I opened the last plastic egg, the watch was in three pieces! Visions of never graduating from middle school flashed before my eyes, and as the Assistant Principal came up to retrieve his watch, I shielded the damage with my hand, and told him in a stage whisper that we would take care of it after the show.

After the show, he came backstage and said, "Don't worry. My watch falls apart all the time." I guess I would be able to go to high school after all.

Mr Mystery!

John and I remained friends, and we performed lots of magic shows together. He loves technology, so he would typically help backstage by working the lights and curtains, playing my music, and helping me with props. In our "Big Show," he became "Alley Oop, the Incredible Caveman Monster," and used a janitor's push broom to sweep props off the stage as a running gag, to the sound of "Little Brown Jug" played by Ken Griffon on the organ.

During the Halloween season, we had so many potential bookings that we couldn't take them all, because some of the schools had their Halloween Carnivals on the same day. That's when we came up with the idea for "Mr Mystery," the masked magician. It was my name in the Yellow Pages that got the bookings, but the posters said, "Mr Mystery," and sometimes Mr Mystery performed at two schools at the same time on the same day.

You've probably guessed that we had two identical costumes, two masks, and two similar shows. The school didn't necessarily know which "Mr Mystery" they were getting...nor did it matter. "Who was that masked man?"

I also sometimes used the Mr Mystery character for our spook shows, which we sold to recreation centers during the sock hop era. We called then "Halloween Hops," or off season simply "Horror Hops." Record hops were often sponsored by Top 40 radio stations, which were eager to promote this idea that distinguished their record hops from others. What can I say...it's magic!

"I'm a Magician!"

I continued performing magic throughout high school, college, and even the military. LSU had mandatory ROTC for all male undergraduate students, so John and I knew that we would be serving in the Army after graduation. And I knew that I was going to marry Margot. At the beginning of June 1965, I went from being an unmarried civilian college student to a married Army Second Lieutenant college graduate.

I wound up staying on active duty for eleven years, serving in Germany, Vietnam, and Korea as well as stateside, and in 1971, the Army sent me to the University of Texas at Austin to get my MBA degree. While in Austin, John Schexnaydre and I started a small restaurant chain called, "the SamWitch shops," with a cartoon witch drawn by my uncle, Jack Kent, as a trademark.

Margot and I fell in love with Austin, came back in 1976, and have lived in this area ever since. We owned and operated our sandwich shop chain for about ten more years, and finally sold them on January 1, 1986, when I officially became a full-time professional magician.

I had long since dropped the "Mysto" moniker as sounding to childish, and became, "The Fantastic Kent Cummins." I liked "fantastic" because it didn't necessarily mean, "great." But it certainly meant interesting! It became a catch phrase as well, so when people ask me how I'm doing, I say, "Fantastic!" What I discovered was that when I said it, I also felt it. My life has truly been fantastic.

Fantastic Magic Camp

I answered the yellow phone on the wall in January, 1993, shortly after my 50th birthday.

"Magic Hotline, this is Kent."

It was a magician from out of town, who had found my name in the Yellow Pages and wanted to hang out and talk magic. I didn't really want to, so I gave him the name of Bobby Cordell, a younger magician who would probably love to do card tricks until the early morning.

But as I hung up, I felt a twinge of guilt. Throughout my life, magicians had always treated me with kindness and respect. And now I didn't have time for a fellow magician? That was my state of mind when I had breakfast with my friend Robert Crampton, a civilian with the Austin Police Department.

Robert worked the McGruff the Crime Dog puppet for APD, and we did shows together called, "McGruff and the Magician." I explained to Robert how I felt bad, and was looking for a way to "give back."

Robert thought about it, and said that if I combined the magic classes I taught at the University of Texas, the puppetry classes that I taught for school counselors, and the juggling workshop that I did for school PE programs, I could have a summer camp.

I said, "That's an interesting idea."

Robert pounded his fist on the table, and said, "No! That's a Business Plan!"

That was in March, and by June "The Magic Camp" was up and running. The camp became a model for inclusion, welcoming kids regardless of any labels they might have, and we eventually developed a Youth Leader Training Academy to teach life skills to the kids when they became teens.

I ran the camp for eighteen years, but when your kids turn 18, you have to let them go. The camp continues, run by people who truly care about the camp. And they renamed it "Fantastic Magic Camp" in honor of the founder.

DISCOVERING THE MAGIC

So what have I learned from all this?

It is said that we create our own reality, and I really believe that this is true. We can't always control what happens in our lives, of course, but we can decide how we are going to react. When I was in the sixth grade, Dad gave me a copy of Norman Vincent Peale's *The Power of Positive Thinking*. The ideas in that book, and more motivational books and tapes since then, have helped me maintain a positive attitude throughout both the good times and the bad.

At a recent gathering of friends in the National Speakers Association, I said that I felt that I had led a charmed life...that I was really lucky...that nothing bad ever happened to me. I said that I almost felt guilty about how easy my life has been.

Debbie Pearson, a friend who is a Registered Nurse with a private case management company, asked me, "What about your mother having a stroke, and your having to care for her?" Someone else pointed out, "What about the year you spent in Vietnam, and nearly got killed?" When I discussed it with Margot, she pointed out the times we had to go to counseling in order to keep our family together.

It is not what happens to us...it is our attitude about whatever happens, and how we choose to deal with it. It's not Hocus Pocus. The magic word is, "ATTITUDE."

I'M GOING TO TELL YOU A SECRET.

Magicians don't usually tell their secrets, but I am going to tell you:

"How to Pull a Rabbit Out of a Hat!"

Are you ready? Do you promise not to tell?

In order to pull a rabbit out of a hat.....you have to put a rabbit into the hat first!

Life is the same way. In order to get what you want out of it, you have to put something into it. The more you study, learn, try new things, make an effort to help others...the more rewarding your own life will be.

You probably never said, "I am going to be a magician." But find the thing that produces magic in your life and in the lives of those around you. Everyone deserves a magical life.

◇◇

"The Fantastic Kent Cummins" is an author, teacher, speaker, juggler...and magician! Kent's first book, **Bungling Juggling***, was published in 1964 by the ELBEE Company while Kent was still in school. In November 2017, a Mini Book reprint of* **The CAN DO Book of Magic** *was published by Magic Words Press. In between, there have been dozens of books and videos, as well as hundreds of newspaper and magazine articles from* **Clowning Around** *to* **Reader's Digest***. Kent has taught magic and juggling classes at the University of Texas for more than thirty years, as well as in hundreds of after school enrichment classes. In 1993, the year that he turned fifty, he started Fantastic Magic Camp, which continues to help children in Central Texas. Kent's specialty is Magic With a Message, in which he uses the fascination and fun of magic to educate and inspire as well as entertain.*

The Divine Download

Lee Moczygemba

About a year after my training business was going well, I became very interested in speaking at conventions and meetings. I knew professional speakers were paid a lot of money, and I wanted to be a real pro in both training and speaking. At age 52 the thought never occurred to me: "You're too old, honey—that boat has already sailed!"

BECOMING A PROFESSIONAL SPEAKER

When I asked myself, "What makes you think you can do this?" my limited, but natural-born confidence answered: "Because I have always been a ham! I have always loved standing before people, telling them stories and making them laugh." (That's literally ALL I had going for me—a strong, deep belief that I COULD do it—if I just knew HOW.)

A wonderful, generous friend came to my rescue. She brought me a copy of Success magazine, and said I might find something interesting that would help me. OH, WOW—DID I EVER! As I was glancing through the last pages, my eyes focused on one particular small ad. I could so easily have missed it! In nondescript print were the words: NATIONAL SPEAKERS ASSOCIATION – SECOND CONVENTION – Phoenix, Arizona – Biltmore Hotel – July 23-25, 1975.

I sprang into action, leaping across the room to the telephone (no cell phones yet), picked it up and dialed the number in the ad. Then a strange thing happened. While listening to the rings, I LOST MY COURAGE. All that wonderful bravado turned to jelly, and negative messages began to flood my head: "Hang up quick! You're not a PROFESSIONAL Speaker! You're about to get in over your head. They'll think you are a fool! You DEFINITELY do not qualify!"

I was just a split second from hanging up when a man answered, and here is exactly what I heard: "N-A-T-I-O-N-A-L S-P-E-A-K-E-R-S A-S-S-O-C-I-A-T-I-O-N, Bill Johnson s-p-e-a-k-i-n. C-a-n I h-e-p ya?" God had placed a "good ole Texas boy" with an unmistakable Texas drawl on that line, and he was an absolute angel to me! When I opened my mouth to answer, I could only squeak. (I was still in shock from all those negative messages in my head.) It was all I could do to introduce myself and tell him I had read the ad. I barely managed to convey I was very, very interested, but just a beginner in professional speaking. I deeply wanted to BECOME a real pro, however.

His exact answer: "C-o-m-e o-n o-u-t, Lee, we'll M-A-K-E o-n-e o-u-t-a ya!!" AND I DID — AND THEY DID!

Wasn't that something? Had he been cold and snobbish, my speaking career would definitely have ended right there. I will never forget his kindness, and how much I appreciated him allowing me to save face.

Before I hung up I committed to attend the convention, and then proceeded to make hotel and airline reservations. I was scared and felt very insecure, but desire was greater than the fear. I didn't know what I was getting myself into. But I wanted to be a speaker with all my heart—and this seemed the best possible way to learn how to be one.

I flew to Phoenix and took a cab to that famous, beautiful, old Biltmore Hotel. As I entered the lobby, I noticed a long table with a big sign: "National Speakers Association Convention." Members and staff were welcoming attendees as they arrived. Bill Johnson was right there, and he came over and welcomed me with a big "Texas-size" handshake. I thanked him for his kindness and encouragement.

The "welcoming committee" told me to put my bags in my room, and then return as quickly as possible. "We have a bus outside waiting to take us to a big rally downtown Phoenix." I was told that in the city coliseum there would be about 19,000 people eagerly waiting to hear some of the greatest speakers in America! We were promised we would have the opportunity to meet each of these celebrities backstage. I was excited!

True to their word, we were introduced to each one separately. (It was all I could do to maintain a fake semblance of poise.) They were all highly successful, very well-known people such as: W. Clement Stone (one of America's early billionaires and a close friend of Napoleon Hill); Art Linkletter, a famous TV star; Paul Harvey, a well-known radio newscaster ("And now you know the rest of the story"); Dr. Robert Schuller, a minister who built the Crystal Cathedral in California; and Zig Ziglar, an extremely popular, charismatic professional speaker.

After meeting those wonderful celebrities, we were ushered into the main auditorium to special reserved seats up front. When the program began, I went into a "Never, Never Land," known as "Camelot," and don't think I have ever quite returned. It was one of the most enchanting experiences of my life. I was in heaven—and found my destiny!

Watching Zig Ziglar is when the epiphany hit me. An inner voice spoke to me with the force like dynamite. It said: "THIS IS WHAT YOU WERE BORN FOR!" Training AND Speaking were my destiny beyond any shadow of a doubt. I knew I was a long, long way from being a "Zig Ziglar," but he had given me the vision of what I COULD become if I were willing to pay the price. I made a vow: "I WILL LEARN TO DO THIS—NO MATTER WHAT IT TAKES!" Finally, I had a clear sense of direction.

The National Speakers Association (NSA) became my guide, and that experience dramatically changed my life. I had the miraculous good fortune of being taught by the masters—not only how to speak, but also how to create a successful business. What a HUGE blessing!

THE SALVATION ARMY

Returning home from "Camelot" was quite a jolt! I was reminded of the day after I left Exxon. The same ole feeling of being alone was overwhelming. My head was crammed full and still spinning with images of all the fascinating people, experiences and learning I had encountered in just three short days. It was so hard to come back down to earth! But once again I heard that little fearful child in me whispering: "I STILL NEED A BOSS! WHAT AM I SUPPOSED TO DO FIRST?" and, " HOW AM I SUPPOSED TO IMPLEMENT ALL THAT WONDERFUL ADVICE I RECEIVED?"

Fortunately, I remembered a previous commitment I had made to speak to the Salvation Army when I returned to Houston. The Major's wife had just completed a speech class I taught and asked if I would be so kind as to come to their offices and give her "boys" an inspirational, motivational talk. She mentioned that they were enrolled in a program that was teaching them valuable life skills.

I readily agreed, but because I was so very busy at the time, inadvertently (shamefully) did not make any effort to interview her and find out specifically who those "boys" were, how they landed in that program, how many "boys" were in the group, and most importantly, what exactly did they need to hear from me?

In my haste to be sure I was properly dressed and arrived on time, I forgot one priceless gem of advice I had learned from the masters at NSA: "Never, Never, NEVER speak to an audience about whom you know practically nothing."

Sooner than expected, the day I was to speak arrived. I put on my "Dress for Success" suit and drove across Houston to "do my thing." I really hadn't planned what I was going to say, but didn't give it a second thought because, by then, I could speak extemporaneously. (Truth is: I had become overly confident.)

The Major's wife met me and was very excited and grateful I had come. She said my audience was eager to hear "this older woman speaker whom she had recommended so highly!" We walked down a long, long hallway and finally stopped before a closed door. Just before opening it, she said, "Here we are! I'm SURE this is going to be a wonderful experience for everyone concerned."

When that door opened, I received one of the biggest shocks of my life. The room was completely filled with thick, blue/grey smoke. About thirty of the gruffest, meanest looking, worst smelling men I have ever seen in my life (each holding a cigarette in one hand and a coffee cup in the other) all stared at me. Despite the heavy fog I could see the looks of skepticism on those faces—as though I were an intruder that definitely did not belong there.

I'm sure I looked equally shocked, if not more so. Nothing in my life had prepared me for what I was walking into. I felt very uncomfortable, but managed to fake a semblance of confidence as I followed the Major's wife. She led me down the center aisle from the back of the room. There was a slightly raised platform, a lectern and a chair to the side. She proceeded to give me a very warm, gracious introduction and then sat down.

Always the eternal optimist, and with that feeble degree of confidence, I pitched in with my high-energy, canned, motivational "Rah Rah Rah" speech. It didn't take but just a few moments before I realized the audience was not with me AT ALL! Truth is, even though I was putting up a brave front, I was scared out of my wits! I realized I was just rambling—and losing them completely. Those men looked like they could eat me alive! NEVER before or since have I EVER faced an audience and felt PURE HATE coming from every single one of them! If was as if they dared me to tell them anything of value! I knew I was in serious trouble.

I had the wrong message for the wrong audience, at the wrong time, at the wrong place! Their contempt and rejection were painfully obvious, and deeply humiliating. Fear began to paralyze me. I realized my lack of preparation was going to cost me big time!

And...I HATE TO LOSE! I hate to lose worse than anything! It never once occurred to me to just walk out and not look back. So I desperately tried to remember something – ANYTHING – the Major's wife had told me about these men.

Vaguely I managed to recall her saying something about them being in a rehabilitation program to help overcome drugs and alcohol. Amazingly, that triggered memories of long ago, stories my father had told me about how wonderful the Salvation Army was in helping people in many, many ways. As a soldier in World War I, he had witnessed he great compassion and generosity of the Salvation Army.

I desperately, FERVENTLY prayed for help—and miraculously received an instantaneous answer. An inner voice shouted: "Take off that coat." So I quickly ditched it, and rolled up my shirt sleeves. Then: "Move away from that lectern, step down and get on the same level with them." I did that immediately!

Standing in the center aisle I heard: "Touch them!" Instinctively and calmly I slowly walked over, reached out, firmly grasped the shoulder of the man who was the meanest looking of them all, held it firmly, and looked him straight in the eyes. He was totally shocked! He stared at me and did not move. Then I was directed: "These men desperately need encouragement and inspiration. Help them!"

My fear totally vanished with those instructions. Now I knew exactly what to do.

Speaking loudly enough for the whole audience to hear, I remember saying: "You men are very brave!" Then I paused, turned my head, and gradually made eye contact with the others—all the way to the back of the room—and then exclaimed: "I CONGRATULATE YOU! You made a difficult, but wise decision when you committed to turning your life around. And you came to the very best place to do that! The Salvation Army has the most wonderful people in the world who are qualified and totally dedicated to helping you find a new and better life. I am SO PROUD OF YOU for making that decision. You have a LOT of courage!"

Then I turned to my right, moved to the other side and, firmly but gently, grasped the shoulder of the man sitting directly across the aisle. (My confidence was now beginning to come back—strong!) I began sharing some of the stories my father had told me, about how some soldiers he knew had changed their lives with the help of the Salvation Army. I looked deeply into this man's eyes intermittently as I spoke to him, as well as maintaining eye contact with the entire group, and when I lifted my hand from his shoulder, I got a big smile!

Somebody "up there"—maybe the Boss Himself—was helping me—big time!

The next instructions were to continue gradually moving down the center isle towards the back of the room—making sure as I spoke—to grasp the shoulder of each of the men in the aisle seats. Allowing myself to be vulnerable, I admitted to them I was fairly sure my outward appearance did not convey signs of the pain and challenges I had endured in my lifetime. I had experienced my own kind of "Hell" and gave an example: "Once I had driven out of the driveway of a lovely home, with my fourteen-month old baby by my side, leaving a marriage and solid financial security. I didn't know how I was going to make a living, survive, and raise that child. I also had to hide from an irate, mean husband who had threatened to kill me if I ever left him!" I told them how I survived and even prospered. Help came from many directions—just as it would come to each of them. God, as well as many good people (angels on this earth), came to my rescue—over and over and over!

I told them I respected and empathized with all the hardships they had endured. Theirs were, no doubt, completely different and most likely much, much worse than mine. I sincerely felt for them, and—once again—complimented them for making the big decision to change. I said I knew it was hard, but they could make a whole new life for themselves if they wanted to with all their heart!

I encouraged them to help each other, live every day with "The Attitude of Gratitude," work as a team, and complete this training program. I reminded them the Major, Ms. Major, and the entire staff genuinely cared about their welfare, and wanted them to succeed.

Gradually—gradually—the "ice began to thaw." They were captivated! They came alive and receptive—listening intensely to every word I was saying.

Then suddenly I realized I had worked myself to the back of the room—and was "all out of soap" (meaning: I didn't know what else to tell them). So, once again I sent up an SOS! I wanted to leave them with something valuable.

And here is the shocking answer I received: "Ask them: 'How many of you can do what I just did—stand up in front of a group of people and speak—hold their attention—and give them a piece of your heart?" Those words came tumbling out of my mouth—and I was as surprised as they were to hear them!

Not a single hand went up, but every set of eyes in the room was staring at me.

Then I was even more shocked with what came out next. Totally spontaneous: "How many of you would LIKE to be able to do that?" EVERY hand went up!

I could not believe I was actually saying the following words: "What if I had permission from the Major to come over here once a week, how many of you would have a sincere interest in learning how to stand up, speak with confidence, and maybe conduct vesper services?" Once again, EVERY hand went up—and the Major's wife smiled and nodded her head vigorously.

I said, "OK, see you next week. I'll find out which day and the time. You promise to show up, and I promise to show up—once a week, every week until you graduate. (I held up my right hand and they all held up theirs.) Is it a deal?

They all stood up, grinning ear to ear, and started clapping! Every one of them.

OMG! What had I just gotten myself into? It was all totally spontaneous—no forethought whatsoever. I had been so intent on wanting to HELP them and give them something of real value, I think I subconsciously came up with speech training because I knew that skill would be a tremendous boost to their confidence and pride. Also, I truly believe that the idea of offering that gift came straight from the Boss Himself!

And THEN I realized I had just created a whole new set of challenges for myself. I had absolutely no way of knowing if I COULD teach these rough, tough, worldly, hardened souls to speak. This would definitely be a leap of faith for me.

Nonetheless, I would give it my best shot! (You know by now I am a born risk-taker, don't you?) Besides, I felt a big payback was due for all that miraculous help I had received in turning around that awful speech!

Out of a miserable mess came a tremendous blessing—for all concerned! And I learned, like never before in my life, the importance of knowing (I mean, REALLY knowing) your audience BEFORE you speak to them!

LEE MOCZYGEMBA is a "late bloomer" who, at age 50, learned to be a very successful International professional speaker and trainer. She left Exxon and gold-plated security to follow her passion, lacking the knowledge and experience necessary. She faced many trials and tribulations before achieving mastery of her craft. This resulted in a deep desire to motivate and inspire others to be confident, successful and happy! Over the years Lee has received several awards for her speaking and training expertise--the most notable: "Lifetime Achievement Award"– National Speakers Association Austin in 2013, and "Mentor of the Year" in 2016 from Woman Communicators of Austin. Ninety-three years young, blessed with a sharp mind, quick wit, and boundless energy, Lee loves life and is still busy coaching ambitious "youngsters" to become professional speakers! The full story of her journey to success, Wake Up–Dress Up–Show Up!, is due for publication in early 2019!!

Resilient Leadership

Dave Swanson

Resilient leadership is a skill learned over time and through experience.

After conducting my interviews, this statement was repeated with unparalleled enthusiasm. I had always known that experience, and practicing resilient leadership, were the keys to being successful—at anything. After attending the United States Military Academy (West Point), I felt that there were certain people who had a tendency to be resilient leaders, an instinct that did not have a quantitative measure nor could be determined at such an early age.

After many years of observation, I have noticed that some people who were not determined leaders at the Academy are now flourishing in the Army today. My interviews were with people who have over 300 plus years of combined leadership experience and that has led me to understand that time, experience and resiliency will make a great leader; having a natural-born gift to be a leader in today's world is simply not enough.

GREAT LEADERS ARE NOT BORN WITH EXPERIENCE.

"Leaders are always developed, never born the way we think they are."
Barry Switzer

Values, Assumptions, Beliefs and Expectations (VABES) are developed over time and through experiences. VABES are shaped by each individual experience and not necessarily one event that determines the ability to lead.

The primary thing that influences leadership is our VABES. It is how we attract other people to us, it shapes how we motivate and drive people. Experiences that shape our VABES ultimately will determine our level of success in the workforce. This could be in a large corporation or in a start-up environment, but VABES will influence every decision, task assignment, and individual work that we will ever do. As a great leader, acknowledging these experiences and sharing them with others will contribute to making other great leaders in other organizations as well.

My personal experience of leading 40 men in combat as an Infantry Platoon leader is not like everyone else's. It wasn't one specific firefight, nor was it the camaraderie that I had with my men. It was all events that led to earning their trust as a leader and in return, them earning mine. My personal VABES, expedited in the course of a year—which I believe would normally take years to develop—were happening in much shorter periods of time because of the environment.

"Upbringing and environment is a big part of the key elements in becoming a leader."
General Deering

LEADERSHIP SKILLS REQUIRE PRACTICE.

"Leadership is the fundamental ability to organize, motivate and inspire other people towards a shared goal; a goal that must be created with others and through a shared vision."
— Vinit Bharara

Through the diamond model of organization structure, practice can be achieved. Through a shared strategy, you, as the leader, assign tasks that require many things to understand.

"Over the years, through a volume of people and personalities and situations will help you reduce conflict, while putting people in positions to be successful. You must understand their areas of strength."
— Harold Kaufman

In addition to the diamond model, working with people and practicing the shared strategy while accomplishing tasks, will allow for the leadership skill set to continuously be enriched.

In my previous experience as a consultant, I worked in a similar organizational structure as the diamond. I had many years of experience in the Army, but only a few in the corporate world and that experience shaped my leadership skills in a profound manner. I had to work within a team, manage a team, and manage expectations that were set by my superiors and clients within the organization.

At first, it was easy to delegate assignments, whoever had free time, would get the task and complete it. Over time, I had to realize skill sets of the employees, I had to learn to react to emotional factors and I had to manage some difficult clients. All of these actions required different skill sets that I did not have at the time. As I practiced my skills as a leader, I became much more equipped to work within that environment as the years continued.

LEADERSHIP AND PRACTICE REQUIRE MENTORS THAT HAVE ALREADY DEVELOPED THAT SKILL.

"Marvin Lewis changed everything, the environment completely changed. He gave out two books on personal management that created a different culture."
— Jeff Berding

Identifying mentors that have already led many people through a variety of experiences can be a challenge. However, it is not impossible to identify yourself with others leadership styles that you want to emulate.

Although not explicitly discussed through the course, mentorship has long been a key to success in many organizations.

"A mentor is someone who helps another person become what that person aspires to be."
— Montreal CEGEP

Mentors shape leaders at every level of the organization from the bottom to the top of the pyramid. At a certain point when a person can become a mentor and still continues to seek mentorship, is what should be strived for because even CEO's of an organization still seeks guidance from others that they respect.

IDENTIFY MENTORS THAT CAN HELP MOLD THE LEADERSHIP SKILL WITH PRACTICE.

"Good leadership styles aren't always universally accepted."
— Wesley Clark

General Clark's observation about leadership is well stated in the sense that finding a great leader for mentorship will not suit everyone. Taking the time to learn about the person who is mentoring you, is just as important as their genuine interest in learning about the person they are mentoring.

Leadership skills are built by experience, but can also be learned through others' experiences. Mentoring is a facilitation of learning from both parties that is invaluable to not only the individuals, but the organization that promotes mentoring groups.

25

> *"I take pride in people that have worked for me, there are 10 people in leading roles within the league and we have a PR tree around the league."*
> — **Harold Kaufman**

Mr. Kaufman's mentoring roles have been able to help many of his former colleagues to aspire to the position that they wanted, which is ultimately, the idealistic goal of mentoring people.

ASSESS LEADERS TO LEARN FROM THEIR MISTAKES.

> *"Soft skills are needed to treat people differently, knowing your people and not giving them the broad brush are the skills I depend on the most."*
> — **Vinit Bharar**

Ultimately, to create a culture for an organization, or in this case, a style of leadership that one looks for when developing their skills.

When assessing great leaders, style is the key to understanding what leadership skills will be the most successful.

> *"I didn't respond to negativity as a player, so I didn't coach that way.
> I got more and my players got more from encouragement, however, recognition
> is only great if it was true. The players knew that."*
> — **Barry Switzer**

Coach Switzer's point on the players being encouraged until they knew it wasn't true is something that has resided with me and my personal development of leadership.

I have learned that my style is to be stricter as a leader, but give praise when it is due and let a person who responds favorably to criticism, to give it, but behind closed doors. Public humiliation as a leader will work for a period of time, until it no longer motivates an individual to achieve their best performance. However, many leaders have found this as a style that suits them and believes it maximizes output of individuals. I have analyzed this of leaders I have been around and it has shaped my style of leadership to what it is today.

People in positions of power don't always have the greatest skill sets for leadership. Based on a previous argument, leadership skills are developed over time and with experiences. People achieve higher levels of power without necessarily have the skills and experiences, but it still continues to happen. There are other VABES at play, there are other theories to attribute to why an individual may reach a position of power over someone else.

In the military, it isn't always easy to identify people who are lacking in leadership skills at the lower levels. Skills will often be discussed in evaluation reports and the results will end up in more training or schooling that will help an individual to gain more experience. In the corporate world, it is very easy to identify someone in a position of power that does not have the required skills to lead. My previous experience would have been to try to quickly identify a path to try and push myself forward to take over that position of power. However, through experiences and my style, I have used my leadership skills to make that person more successful.

SEEK OUT LEADERS THAT FIT YOUR PERSONALITY.

Organizations that have great shared values, have great leaders that created that type of culture. Mr. Berding's comment on his thoughts of the owner and how he is a leader that he wants to imitate fits his personality. Through that specific experience, his leadership skills and knowledge have grown to create a culture within his division, to mimic the owner's behavior.

Seeking out leaders that have similar shared values will create a framework for understanding what is necessary in developing an individual's leadership skills.

In my experiences since leaving the military, it hasn't always been easy to identify the culture of the organization. It has typically taken about months to years, to truly understand the behaviors of people within a company. I have also taken positions where the leader has established the shared values of the organization from the outset in the interview. This has been the best style I have seen yet, when it comes to sharing what to expect of a company. In the future, I will establish shared values discussion early, let people know about my style of leadership and discuss my skills and experiences with the individuals in the organization.

REGARDLESS OF BACKGROUND,
LEADERSHIP IS REQUIRED AT ALL LEVELS OF MANAGEMENT.

> *"Leadership is always about understanding the context of a situation and working within that context. Be, know, do – Army Values that apply to all ethical dilemmas as a junior officer and at the top level."*
> — **Wesley Clark**

General Clark's statement applies to the US Army, but successful leadership can not only be at the top of a company.

The configuration of an organization must have great leaders from the top of the structure through the middle managers and at the bottom. The structure of emplacing leaders with credentials at all levels is actually more of a challenge than understood. Much of this, can be described by staffing, however, beyond staffing the right team of leaders, the structure needs to be sound enough for the organization to focus on this.

LEADERSHIP IS A SKILL THAT EVERY MANAGER NEEDS.

> *"Politics and pro sports are very similar. In politics, you have an election, there are no do-overs, and we worked as a team and got it done. Football is the same way, you're going to be tested, and you either win or lose."*
> — **Jeff Berding**

From conceptual skills to human skills, there will be times that leadership will be required (organizational missions, strategies) and times that being a manager is required by implementing these missions and strategies.

Leadership and management are interchanged quite frequently when it comes into discussion. The discussion is that it is simply broken up by one who assigns tasks and one who establishes a vision. I propose that leadership is a skill that goes beyond management. When it is practiced, it is sharpened over time and through experiences. In today's corporate world, those that ultimately succeed have the ability to do both when it is required of them.

When it came to combat, I understood what I was asking of the men in my platoon. I used to be that soldier in my platoon and that gave me credibility with the soldiers, which led to trust at its highest level. My leadership skills grew dramatically between the times of being an E-1 (the lowest enlisted grade) to where I became an O-1 (the lowest commissioned officer grade). I attended the United States Military Academy, I went through various courses of training at Fort Benning, Georgia, and I had been out to other units to train and observe. Only seven years had passed within that time frame, but I had learned that leadership was a skill that is needed at all levels.

> *"I made the mistakes as a younger manager – brash, cocky, had all the answers.*
> *I corrected people with arrogance and I disagreed with our marketing executive*
> *and micromanaged. Over time, she was ineffective because of my management style.*
> *I learned patience through that position."*
>
> **—Vinit Bharara**

Mr. Bharara's comment is not a surprise to people who have had to lead other individuals at such an early age. Peer leadership and leading individuals who are older with more experience is one of the most challenging positions of power to have within an organization.

As I became a platoon leader as an Officer, my style had drastically changed. I was more laid back and the first time I spoke in front of the platoon, I had already garnered the support of my Platoon Sergeant (13 years' experience) and several others whom I had discussions with that yielded their support. I didn't make any bold statements and I stated that I would take the time to get to know all of them over the next few weeks. Through my actions and my genuine concern to get to know all of my soldiers, I garnered a great rapport with the platoon in a much shorter time than when I was younger.

> *"Treat everyone with respect. Surround yourself with the best people possible.*
> *Good people make good things happen and show them loyalty. Personally care*
> *for each person on the team and that will make you successful."*
>
> **— Barry Switzer**

CONSTANTLY HONE LEADERSHIP SKILLS WITH PRACTICE AND ANALYSIS OF OTHER LEADERS.

> On the leadership skills he depends on the most: *"Character, commitment,*
> *communication, collaboration, confidence, consistency, caring, and culture."*
>
> **— General Deering**

Major General Deering's statement lays out systematic framework for how to be a leader in organization.

> *"The emphasis of communication in a system cannot be stressed enough."*
>
> **— General Deering**

Through honing leadership skills and analyzing other great leaders, an individual's leadership style will be formed over time. As an individual is working on skills and practicing, creating a system and culture that fosters that environment is an idealistic approach for any organization.

I have consistently honed my leadership skills and analyzed other leaders throughout the military and my career in the corporate world. This is commonly taught at West Point as a way to perfect leadership skills. I have often found that while not only practicing my skills, I have analyzed other leaders, both good and bad to find out what works. As I have moved several companies, I have recognized that there are going to be challenges of managers at every level. It could be in other departments, it could be with peers, subordinates, but there are going to be those at every organization. After this recognition, I observe and learn what people are responding to that makes them more effective, and also find out what drives individual's motivation away.

In summary, my reflection on going through the process of interviewing and networking has been career changing. I have had the chance to interview some of the most charismatic leaders of our lifetime and I have also had the experience of meeting some people who I would have never had the chance to discuss leadership.

After conducting the interviews, I fully believe that leadership is a skill learned over time and through experiences. We are not simply born with the ability to lead individuals without having experiences to guide us. Leadership requires practice, it requires mentorship to learn, and time in leadership roles is crucial to the development of a leader.

Bios:

General Wesley Clark (Ret) – Wesley Kanne Clark, Sr. is a retired General of the United States Army. He graduated as valedictorian of the class of 1966 at West Point and was awarded a Rhodes scholarship to the University of Oxford, where he obtained a degree in Philosophy, Politics and Economics.

Coach Barry Switzer – Barry Switzer is a former football coach. He spent sixteen years as head coach of the University of Oklahoma and four years as head coach of the Dallas Cowboys, winning 3 National Championships and 1 Super Bowl.

Vinit Bharara – Vinit Bharara was previously the General Counsel of the then publicly traded The Topps Company, Inc, the leading manufacturer of sports trading cards and novelty confectionery (e.g., Bazooka gum and Ring Pop, Push Pop and Baby Bottle Pop).

General Myles Deering – Myles Lynn Deering is an Army National Guard major general who currently serves as the Adjutant General of Oklahoma.

Harold Kaufman – Harold Kaufman brings more than 25 years of publicity and media relations experience to the Mets organization.

Jeff Berding - 17 years as an Executive and a Director of Sales & Public Affairs with the Cincinnati

Bengals, goal is to have stadium 100% sold out and to have team win the Super Bowl. He is currently President of FC Cincinnati soccer team.

◇◇

Dave Swanson is a motivational speaker with an incredible background as a US Army Infantry platoon leader who engaged in over 100 firefights while deployed to Sadr City, Iraq. Dave is a consummate leader who speaks with a sense of humor that reminds us that we all have the resiliency to overcome all obstacles. Dave's background includes:

A distinguished career as an Army Officer and a Bronze Star Medal recipient
2016 Recipient of Dean's Leadership and Service Award for the McCombs School of Business for the MBA program
Reached the summit of Mt. Ranier
Bicycled 3100 miles across America to raise money for several Non-Profits in 30 days
Currently pursuing his Ph.D. in Leadership
Has spoken for many Fortune 500 companies on leadership
The author of The Dot on the Left

Get More Gigs!
Converting Decision Makers into Paying Clients

Donn LeVie, Jr.

Every speaker, coach, and consultant wants to book higher paying gigs. For some, the biggest challenge is simply picking up the phone and talking to a decision maker. For others, it's a matter of settling on exactly what to say. I'm going to share with you several approaches I've used successfully to book keynotes and seminars at conferences around the country. It's simple and it doesn't cost anything: The secret is to keep decision makers talking by asking questions and planting strategic responses that, in turn, encourage them to continue asking questions. Getting to the kernel of challenges, issues, and problems of others helps both parties see more clearly the path to resolution. The deeper you both go with conversation, the higher the odds of your approach being the only viable solution, and converting that decision maker into a paying client.

Rinse and repeat...until you've addressed all their concerns, then close the deal with a final question that begins with something like: "Is there any reason we can't move forward now to...(book a speaking or seminar gig, sign a contract, schedule a program)?"

Whether you're promoting your expertise for the first time to a potential client, a potential customer, or a meeting professional, it's helpful to first pique their curiosity with a statement that begs for more information. I do that with a value proposition lead-in statement. We use value propositions every day for a variety of situations at work with coworkers and at home with family members. It's a statement that anticipates the tangible, functional reasons (or questions) any decision maker (manager, spouse, angry neighbor) may have for buying from you, hiring you, or simply considering your proposed solution to a problem they have.

Such questions might include the following:

- What does your service/product/expertise/solution mean for me?

- Why should I buy this product/service or hire you over all others being considered?

- How is your expertise/product/service/solution different from others being considered?

Others call a value proposition an "elevator pitch" where you have 20 to 30 seconds to explain your value and expertise to someone in an elevator when asked, "What do you do?" Some liken the value proposition to what you can write on the back of your business card. That brief statement must testify to you or your business being that problem-solving, solutions-providing, game-changing entity decision makers have been looking for.

The problem with most value propositions is that they are encased in convoluted, formal-sounding language, or are written in such a manner that usually fail to invite dialogue...because, that's what you're after: establishing dialogue to continue a conversation. All too often value propositions sound like dead-end statements that fail to encourage continuing the conversation, or they sound too self-serving rather than other serving.

WEAPONS OF INFLUENCE

Dr. Robert Cialdini, in his hugely successful book, *Influence: The Psychology of Persuasion,* refers to six categories of psychological influence principles as "weapons of influence": Consistency, reciprocation, social proof, authority, likability, and scarcity. These principles, when applied by skilled practitioners, direct human behavior in an almost automatic manner in response to requests for purchases, donations, concessions, votes, access, and so on.

A lead-in statement preceding a value proposition can serve as social proof of your value and expertise; it can provide a stamp of authority to a service you provide; it can highlight a limited but needed skill; and it can push open the door to high-fee speaking/consulting/coaching engagements.

THREE examples of winning value propositions

WHAT HAPPENS IN VEGAS . . .

In late December of 2016, I was the guest of a guest for a client appreciation weekend over New Years in Las Vegas, courtesy of one of the large casino resorts. One afternoon, members of the casino resort C-suite came out to meet our small group. I met one of the vice-presidents and after exchanging greetings and some small talk, he asked me: "Donn, what is it that you do?"

I responded with my carefully crafted value proposition lead-in: "Association executives and meeting professionals hire me to make them look like Super Stars…"

He smiled and followed up with the Golden Question that invites dialogue: "How do you do that?"

It was only after I set the hook that I responded with my value proposition:

"My customized professional development keynotes and seminars are outcome-based events. They help associations do a better job with their marketing to get more members, retain members, and discover non-dues revenue approaches…"

He continued the conversation with another question: "How do your programs do that?"

"My programs give attendees the strategy, tactics and tools to engage decision makers, position their branded expertise, and use their value to influence decision makers to convert them to clients and customers. All my programs include coordinated follow up with attendees with additional content to ensure new strategies, tactics, and mindsets take hold.

"My programs are a great investment in conference ROI, they help push the Return on Event through the roof…and get members to return to event the following year."

(I've practiced this value proposition enough times that it sounds like natural conversation because I don't memorize it word for word, but do so in blocks or chunks of ideas that still gets the point across.)

The vice-president's comeback: "We need to talk.… we need to get you in front of some of our teams."

He then called over other C-suite members where the conversation turned into a group discussion. I immediately followed up by asking them questions to determine their organization's needs and issues. My objective was to see how and where I could help, not sell them a seminar program or keynote. I came off looking like someone who had a fix for their specific issues, not a peddler of services. To sweeten the deal, I sent those C-suite members copies of my career strategy books.

The same situation occurred the next evening over dinner with a group of directors and vice-presidents from another large casino resort. I happened to be seated next to the associate vice-president of sales, and again, I was asked the same questions, I provided the same responses, and I enjoyed the same result.

I doubt that the direction those conversations took would be the same if I answered the "what do you do?" question with: "I speak to associations on engagement and influence strategies and write books on the subject." Such a response just wouldn't steer the conversation in the direction I wanted it to go.

KEEPING CLIENTS OUT OF JAIL

Jim McConnell, corporate security professional out of the Dallas, Texas area, attended my program on "Positioning Your Anti-Fraud Expertise" at the 2017 Global Fraud Conference in Nashville, Tennessee. Jim says:

"I immediately implemented one of your many nuggets: 'How do you do that?' and changed my LinkedIn tag line and vocal lead-in statement to: 'I keep my clients off the front page, keep executives alive and out of jail, and make suppliers accountable.'"

That is a great setting-the-hook statement.

With a lead-in statement like that, you can't help but ask: "How do you do that?" Here's Jim's value proposition:

"Domestic and international clients want my converged-security expertise that integrates fraud prevention/deterrence and physical/personnel/cyber security applications that offer full-circle protective measures."

He could follow up that value proposition with: "If you have a few minutes, I'd be happy to share with you how this works for my clients . . ."

Time to reel in the catch.

FINDING VALUE IN A SINGLE WHEAT SEED

Several months ago, I spoke to a church men's group here in Austin, Texas. As I was mingling with the men afterwards, I noticed a sharply dressed African-American gentleman named Don walking among the crowd and handing individuals a small plastic packet containing a single wheat seed. This piqued my curiosity so I edged closer to listen.

Don would approach one of the men, introduce himself and state, "I have a gift for you..." and then he handed them the plastic packet containing the single wheat seed. Nearly everyone to the man asked, "What's this for?" Don responded with another question: "Are you familiar with John 12:24, the parable of the wheat seed?" And before anyone could answer, Don would continue, "When the wheat seed is buried, it regenerates into a bountiful harvest..."

As I observed Don, I thought to myself: "This guy's approach is brilliant!" As I introduced myself to him, he explained to me that the story of the regenerated wheat seed is the foundation for his life's work running a non-profit organization called Regeneration House. Regeneration House is two group homes in Austin that help men transition from various rehab programs for additions, behaviors and the prison experience, to a regenerated life devoid of such distractions, destruction, and dangers.

I was impressed by Don's set up, value proposition, his high likability factor, and his master of impression management language so much so that I am now Chairman of the Board for Regeneration House. But I also believe in Don's mission for getting these men to become better husbands, fathers, and sons for their families and communities.

The set up and value proposition together help you locate, connect with, and even attract others who are looking and listening for something or someone offering value for them. For me, I was looking for ways to be more active in giving back to my community.

I never thought I would find that value through a single wheat seed in a plastic packet.

VALUE PROPOSITION FOR A CONSULTANT

Let's look at using a value proposition lead-in for a consultant seeking to add a new client company.

(Decision maker): "So, tell me Tom...why should we bring you in instead of anyone else?"

(Tom's lead-in): "Mr. Jones, companies like yours hire me because of the future benefits my proven problem-solving expertise will bring to the strategic objectives of the organization."

(Hiring manager/decision maker): "How do you do that?"

(Tom's value proposition): "My successes with other corporate clients in loss prevention demonstrate my ability with not only recovering more than $X in revenues, but that knowledge and skill set will contribute to the ongoing business goals of your enterprise...from Day 1. What would be your highest priority project that I could help with immediately?"

Tom lays out his value proposition and ties it in with suggesting to the decision maker that he's the only logical candidate to receive the consulting contract with his question. Tom doesn't leave anything to chance or dead air as he probes the decision maker with more questions that further reveal his expertise as a value-add problem solver.

VALUE PROPOSITION FOR SALES/TRAINER

Let's next look at using a value proposition lead-in for someone representing an enterprise seeking a new customer or client.

(Decision maker): "Tell me something about your company, Diane."

(Diane's lead-in): "Mr. Jones, HR recruitment directors like you hire us to help them sleep better at night…"

(Decision maker): "How exactly do you do that?"

(Diane's value proposition): "Our Talent Spotting and Onboarding training program is not only the most preferred solution for talent management acquisition and retention, it gives you that worry-free cross-reference capability, real-time candidate offer and onboard activity tracking, and 24/7/365 phone support that includes upfront training and three-month on-site software support. Let me ask you: What other pressing recruiting or retention issues are keeping you up at night?"

Diane takes the same approach as Tom does in the previous example by presenting herself and her company as problem solvers, not a peddlers of HR recruitment training and software. She knows the pain point of the decision maker: Worrying ("losing sleep") about real-time candidate offer and onboard activity tracking and on-site support availability. She jumps in by demonstrating through questions that she wants to help solve problems.

Another approach to the "How do you do that?" question is to answer it with another question: "You know how…?

(Client/decision maker): "How do you do that?"

(You): "You know how…(state the problem or issue the decision maker may have) …? Well, what we do (or what I do) is…(explain how your product, service, expertise solves that problem uniquely). Tap into that customer pain and lead them out of their suffering to the Promised Land.

Here's a simple formula for creating a value proposition:

Target audience + Category + Functional/Symbolic/Experiential Benefit(s) + Reason to Believe

To (Target audience) + our/my (Product or Service category) + is the (Functional/ Symbolic/Experiential benefit) + that provides + (Functional/Symbolic/Experiential benefit) + because + (Reason to believe).

To loss prevention specialists in the retail clothing industry, our wireless HD microcamera security system is the most preferred electronic surveillance device that provides fail-safe, worry free security assurance because of 100% uptime, triple-redundant backup servers, and 24/7 support.

USING "PRE-SUASIVE" QUESTIONING TO HELP SEAL THE DEAL

Author Robert Cialdini explains in *Pre-Suasion: A Revolutionary Way to Influence and Persuade* how to exploit the critical window of time before delivering an important message. This "privileged moment for change", as Cialdini calls it, makes others receptive to a message before they experience it. Peak persuasion happens only through peak pre-suasion. The challenge, then, to change minds is to pre-suade by first changing states of mind.

Here are some example questions that have pre-suasion built into them. The state-of-mind change implied in these questions is that the inquirer already has received some upfront agreement (perhaps on the value that can be delivered) from the decision maker; it's just a matter of determining the priority or pain point to address first.

"What is your second greatest priority/issue and how else do you see my addressing it?"

"What other outcomes do you envision for the event/organization, and how do you see me adding value there?"

"Do you have any other questions or concerns I can address right now about how I can help make your event more successful?"

"If you don't have any other questions of me, is there any reason why we can't move forward with a signed contract?"

"If you don't have any other questions, I have just one more: Since this program will really move the needle for your attendees/employees/managers, are you committed to make the results happen with this program, or are you just interested in it?" (Credit for this one goes to my speaker marketing coach, David Newman, CSP).

ENCOUNTERING RESISTANCE FROM DECISION MAKERS

Who hasn't encountered resistance from a decision maker at one time or another? Having the value discussion before the investment discussion (don't call it a "fee") can mitigate hesitation and resistance. One approach I've used to circumvent decision-maker pushback is to focus on the decision maker's pain or fear of loss, as suggested in these example lead-ins:

"What are you going to do next time when…(something bad happens, with the implication that you can prevent it today)? Because we can solve it once and for all, we can solve it right – how does that sound?"

"From now on, what will you say when…(something bad happens, with the implication that you can prevent it today)? Because we can solve it once and for all, we can solve it right –– how does that sound?"

"What will you do in the future when…(something bad happens, with the implication that you can prevent it today)? Because we can solve it once and for all, we can solve it right – how does that sound?"

Check out speaker marketing guru David Newman's website at www.doitmarketing.com to download his Do It! Marketing Manifesto.

FINAL THOUGHTS

Regardless of what you call yourself on your business card, you are a professional "solver" of other people's problems and issues. There's only one underlying reason a decision maker will chose to do business with you or hire you: You help them get something of value they want or need. It's never about you; it's always about them.

It's clear that a well-constructed lead-in statement and value proposition improve your value position with decision makers. They create the conditions for continued dialogue where you can elaborate on the value of your programs, dig deeper into conversations to uncover additional program opportunities, and lay the groundwork for that high-fee speaking, consulting, or seminar engagement.

Keynote speaker, seminar leader, positioning/influence strategist, and award-winning author Donn LeVie Jr. (donnleviejrstrategies.com; donnleviejrspeaking.com) shows audiences how to build successful, rewarding careers and businesses in a variety of industries. Donn has nearly 30 years' experience in hiring manager/project manager positions for Fortune 100 companies (Phillips Petroleum, Motorola, and Intel Corporation), has been a NOAA research oceanographer, and adjunct faculty lecturer (Department of Natural Sciences and Mathematics), at the University of Houston Downtown College.
Donn is the author of Confessions of a Hiring Manager Rev. 2.0 (Second Edition), *2012 WINNER of the International Book Award (IBA) and 2012 GOLD MEDAL WINNER of the Global eBook*

Award (GeBA) for Careers. He is also the author of Strategic Career Engagement: The Definitive Guide for Getting Hired and Promoted, *2016 IBA RUNNER-UP and 2016 GeBA SILVER MEDAL WINNER for Careers. Donn holds a B.S degree in Geology with graduate work in geochemistry, and is a Certified Fraud Examiner (CFE).*

 Ready to give your conference attendees the unfair advantage in their career and business trajectory? Watch what others say about the value Donn's programs provide and learn how his positioning and engagement strategies can help push conference Return on Event through the roof.

 Download the E.P.I.C Results© Program brochure to schedule a half-day or deep-dive full-day program with Donn LeVie Jr.

What's the Next Conversation?

Teri Hill, M.Ed

We have more methods of communicating than ever: social/mobile, email, text, Twitter, Facebook, v-blogs, and more. Yet communication is not improving. Ask any company, big or small, for their #1 issue and they'll readily tell you it is communication. Ask any struggling couple what broke down in their relationship and 70% say it is communication. Ask parents what they would like more of with their children you will hear: "quality communication."

Communication is a massive structure consisting of several elements. Let's break it down to an element level. How can we guide individuals and teams in defining and conducting quality conversations that move us all further and faster while building stronger, more trusting relationships?

What is Conversation?

Conversations in the present context refer to dialogue or group conversation to get at the root cause of a problem, resolve an issue, express a need or request, all while enhancing the relationship and building trust. The quality of our conversations, in person and especially over media, have diminished in both driving results and building relationship. Conversations go awry for a variety of reasons including poor listening, interruptions, tangents, excessive details, poor construction of thoughts, vocal or visual distractions, on and on.

The intent of this chapter is to explore the subtle, insidious reasons conversations falter.

Many things have occurred that disrupt our ability to hold quality conversations. The mass velocity of change encouraging "life hacks" or shortcuts to try to get to the end result faster.

Our focus on learning the art of conversation, rules of decorum and etiquette have gone by the wayside. Education on basic timing and tenor of a quality conversation that once was learned by watching our elders is diminishing. Below are reasons why conversations are important to pursue, are challenging to hold, and techniques to improve our capacity for enhancing relationships while rapidly delivering solutions, resulting in moving your business and life forward faster.

How do you know a conversation is indicated? What is the landscape to work from in having the conversation? What are some tips, techniques to assist in gaining clarity on what to say and what not to say? How do you avoid getting triggered and taken away from the outcome of getting both what you need in the conversation while also building strength and trust in the relationship.

The focus here is on the effective conversations in the business world. Not at a macro, political, economic level but at a level of enhancing understanding and moving forward in a collaborative way to get things done at a higher rate of speed and enhanced quality.

What are some of the signs present in organizations that a conversation needs to be had?

- People talk around issues with people who don't directly impact the issue or outcome. Call it gossip, water cooler talk, complaining, blaming, or the spiffed-up version of complaining: venting. This banter happens with anyone except the person with whom it would be most advantageous to converse with.

- Attempting to gather allies to support your side of a "perceived" disagreement or uncomfortable conversation. We all seek to validate our assumptions. Before we know it the assumptions are the thing that is most real and we've lost touch with the real observed data, problem, or issue.

- Avoiding the person with whom you really need to be holding a quality conversation. This includes: going out of the way so you won't walk near the person that you really need to talk with; long stints of amnesia about what needs to be said followed by brief insights of "missed opportunities" to talk to the person with whom a conversation is indicated."

- Waiting or hoping that someone else will have the conversation. This is frequently accompanied by fantasies that the person will miraculously find out what you would like for them to know.

One can see how the consequences of this practice waste time while potentially eroding relationships. The cost is seen in wasted time as well as mounting frustration. In an atmosphere as high in velocity as our current competitive business environment, we can't afford to waste time or erode business relationships. The final obnoxious consequence?

Putting grandiose policies, procedures, or business practices in place to control the rogue behavior of one or two individuals when all that is needed is a conversation. This habit of taking issues a galaxy too far stifles performers, wastes precious time and sucks resources that could be used more creatively. Punitive attendance or late polices come to mind. Most people get the work done in a timely manner. Some overachieve. Few need suffocating corporate policies to dictate timeliness. Pay people for performance, not merely attendance.

When we avoid holding corrective conversations or even enlightening conversations for fear the other person may be offended, upset, resentful, defensive, or even combative, we miss the opportunity to build relationships, solve issues, enhance our own perspectives, and move things along quicker. We also lose moral and intellectual credibility.

Another poisonous consequence of avoiding conversations is the reinforcement of cultures built around blame, denial, fault finding, avoidance, and stagnation. These practices cripple future honesty and build the muscle memory of avoidance. Shying away from holding corrective or difficult conversations is a subtle, incestuous, often unconscious, and easily missed problem in our society.

WHY ARE CONVERSATIONS SO DIFFICULT?

There's a deep question. There are natural barriers to communicating that are present in our society. Each of these barriers goes deep and matter greatly. Truth is we are all different and that impacts our ability to hold effective conversations. These differences impact our ability to speak so we are understood. Differences impact how we grasp the message, develop meaning, define next steps of action, and impact trust and accountability. Realistically, there are numerous challenges in communicating effectively. Consciously or unconsciously people avoid taking the time to hold a conversation even though it can dramatically accelerate momentum in business, gain collaboration, harness alignment, create mutual end goals, solve problems, drive accountability, and move past barriers all while enhancing relationship and trust.

Perhaps it doesn't occur to you that a conversation is the next, best step. I strongly assert that it is not just a conversation but the right conversation that is shared from an intention of solution, forward momentum, and desire for mutual advancement in both relationship as well as results.

"The problem with communication is the illusion that it has occurred."
— George Barnard Shaw

Person A may believe they are being clear and to them perhaps the topic, intent of message, and delivery mode makes perfect sense. Unfortunately, person B, C, or D may not follow the flow, understand the intent, or be comfortable with the delivery. This stops the effectiveness of communicating through conversation. What creates this?

- Family of origin. The first place we learn the guidelines of conversation is from our families. Styles of discussion, topics considered discussable, patterns of speech vocal and visual may differ wildly from one another. In my family of origin some topics were not to be discussed: money and sex come to mind. Religion and politics were also considered topics to be tread on lightly. Any topics causing conflict were to be avoided. I recall the familiar reprise- "If you don't have anything nice to say don't say anything at all." And the stifling- "Children are to be seen and not heard." I don't quite recall when we were supposed to turn into young people with something to say. Heaven forbid that our opinion may hurt someone's feelings. Some families, my Italian/Irish friends, were quite vocally, visually, and verbally animated. They not only said what was on their mind but often would shout it with gestures that could chase mountain lions away.

- Personality Traits. The beauty of being human is we are created uniquely. We see the world from different perspectives based on traits like Intuition, Extraversion, Resilience, Originality, Logic, Caution, Desire for Change vs. Stability, Linear vs. Global thinkers. Each personality style has layers of sub styles. Intelligence level, the amount of "gut instinct" or street smarts that a person will use in their reasoning skills varies. How much time someone needs to think about a topic before they can even formulate words around that topic varies drastically. Yet too often we assume everyone thinks like we do and therefore our approach will resonate with them or incite action. Recognize we foster stronger solutions by engaging the different styles. Realize it may take time to understand the varied style of others and they need time to truly understand you.

  It is difficult to communicate in a manner that other people readily understand and can quickly respond in a manner that moves the topic forward. Too often we can get stuck misunderstanding, stop listening in an attempt to push our own agenda, or get triggered into a defensive reaction.

- Generational differences. This behemoth issue has been the topic of hundreds of articles, books, blogs, and dinner table conversations, and has turned into a handy excuse for not believing that it is possible to get through to someone. Generational differences have become the politically correct version of racial or sexual differences. How many times in the past month have you heard someone complain about Millennials?

- Ethnicity or country of origin. Our ethnic/country of origin differences impact what we consider to be discussable and un-discussable topics. It impacts our view of the world and of possibilities. Some people were raised in strong family units, making collaborative decisions while others operated under an authoritative regime where freedom was stifled. Some people grew up in a community of competition and intense work focus while others had more lenience and free time to explore options.

- Male verse Female. Need I say more? Not only are the genders hardwired differently but historically they have been socialized to believe different rules apply in business, negotiation, competition, placement in society, and ability to influence. Many people forget that until very recent, a large % of women in the world didn't even have the right to vote.

- Belief Systems. There are born optimists and born pessimists. People who see the glass as half full and those who see it half empty. Some of this is personality style, some genetic, some family or origin. Much of this is programmed into us at a very early age (birth to 7 years) before we had the maturity to make conscious choices or evaluate the message. Fortunately, there exists a science around altering belief systems. Many people benefit from renewal in inherent belief systems; particularly if they want to be successful in holding quality, impactful conversations.

The strongest, yet most elusive barrier to holding quality conversations is based on science or neuro-chemical brain impulses. Natural, biological responses that people have when they are triggered by something that threatens them impact the trajectory of most modern conversations. The most primal part of our brain, the amygdala gets lit up or stimulated when we are triggered by something that we perceive as being a threat to our immediate well being.

Some people are highly tuned in becoming very reactive when triggered while others are more resilient; they slow down and take information in at a reduced pace, needing to process it mentally before they are ready to discuss. Highly reactive people tend to comprise the 'fight' in the classical fight or flight styles. Their amygdala hijacks neuro-impulses or shuts down signals to the neocortex (the logical, reasonable thinking part of the brain). A trigger can be a word or phrase that causes the other person to leap to an assumption about the intent of the person talking. During an amygdala hijack the lack of stimuli in our neocortex coupled by the abundance of stimuli in our amygdala— the primal brain or seat of emotion, stimulates a reaction in the body that feels like a threat to safety. Adrenaline starts pumping, pulse rate increases, and blood flows away from the brain toward the muscles. If we perceive our safety is threatened, we tend to fight or flee to a safer place. Generally, this happens mentally since we have been programmed not to run from the room in terror or strangle the "threat" in the act of self- protection.

This part of the conversation is where people start to lash out, get defensive, go off topic, stall or stop listening and start to push back to protect themselves. Often the "threat" is not real but the conversation gets derailed and can disintegrate going off topic or escalating into agitation or anger. A small difference in opinion may escalate into a self-protective monologue.

As a consultant I see this happen quite often. It takes education and self-awareness to recognize this biological barrier. It takes hours of practice to reign it in and move past it, back into the flow of effective conversation.

The process of holding effective conversations

Effective conversations start with preparation and awareness. There are three main process steps: Proactive Personal Insight, Pre-conversation Prep, and Conversation Flow. Below are the two most critical.

Proactive Personal Insights:

- Know thyself. The more you understand about your own tendencies in conversation, your own personality, your style under stress, your triggers, and your strengths the better you will be able to navigate conversations. It is critical to understand where a difference in styles, generations, reactions, reasoning, etc. is occurring and if you know your own style you can more readily discern the style of others. You also will be able to OWN your part in either moving the conversation along or disrupting it.

- Know others. Simply recognize that we are all uniquely designed, have unique tendencies, and varied needs or agendas. Stop to assess how others may think, perceive, or feel about issues.

- Know we all tell ourselves stories. These stories about how others think or react may not be real. We all make assumptions. We see something and tell ourselves a story about why it occurred or what motivated the action or reaction. When we tell ourselves a story we look for information to validate our assumptions, real or unreal. Soon we have mentally drifted from the actual incident, evidence, or data and are simply making stuff up (stories).

This mental model was first defined by psychologist Chris Argyris in the 1980s. He likens this tendency to going up a ladder where the rung before feeds the next rung. We start with directly observable data or real evidence and select pieces of that data/experience. Next, we assign meaning to the pieces of evidence we have paid attention to; often determining if it is a threat to us or not. Next, we make an assumption about the motive of the other person. This is followed by coming to conclusions about the person based on the assumed motive. "It must be this way." Or "This is the reason or their motive." Then we look for ways to affirm and preferentially pay attention to the ideas or actions that validate our assumptions.

The consequence is that we get so far off the real incident we start to behave like our stories or assumptions dictate, not what the evidence shows to be true. This drastically skews our conversations, both content and style.

Pre-Conversation Prep — Clear, Centered & Vulnerable

Get clear. What is the end result you desire? To share expectations on a project? To define roles or expectations in making something happen? Or clarification on what next step is going to occur? Do you need to have someone hear you out, listen to what is frustrating you or stalling progress? Do you want the conversation to result in information that cascades through the organization or just stays with- in the confounds of the discussion?

Get clear on what impact you intend to have on the relationship with the person. Are you looking to encourage them to generate ideas? Take the next step of action? Or do you want to show them that you are supportive of their decisions? Create an intention, a goal for the relationship because you will impact the relationship whether you are clear or not. It is always best to keep the focus on enhancing trust and building confidence in others.

Get into a habit of being centered and calm before you get into a conversation. Fill your mind with positive expectations, picture a positive outcome. Like an Olympic Athlete preparing to ski down a slope; go through a ritual in your head, picturing every turn, visualizing the slope, the outcome, and feeling the sensations of successful execution before you ever leave the shoot. Athletes know to do this from a calm place. It is always best to have conversations, particularly crucial conversations where tensions run high and opinions vary, when you are calm and content. Remember the amygdala hijack. Primal brain takes over when we are overly tired, overly hungry, agitated, stressed, hurried, or otherwise upset.

Get vulnerable. Realize that people will be more open with you if you are genuine and open with them. Too often, especially young leaders think that they need to assert, demand, or command respect. Respect is earned through action that is in alignment with values and produces positive results, not by being the strongest or the smartest, and certainly not by shutting down the other person in a conversation.

CONCLUSION

It is personal choice, not circumstance that determines our fate. Choose to recognize the dynamics in conversation, pause and get centered so you can make a conscious choice. Believe that faster results and stronger relationships are built on mutual respect, discovery of truth, and the blended flow of quality conversations. We are tribal people at our core. We once had only conversation to pass on information, build consensus and thrive. We can get back to our roots.

Teri Hill, M.Ed. president of T.H.Enterprise has been consulting, coaching and speaking for over 25 years. She has led in the facilitation of global executive education, trained and coached thousands of leaders, entrepreneurs and rising stars. A former executive, Teri understands the challenges in hiring, effective team communication, cultures of accountability, leading and retaining people. Teri's passion is balanced between speaking to educate and inspire, coaching to fast track development, and consulting to facilitate the profitable growth of small- mid size business, the backbone of America. Teri is a Trusted Advisor and Expert Speaker for Vistage, a leading Chief Executive Association; facilitator of accelerated leadership programs and business masterminds; she has held numerous professional BOD positions, including Past President of Austin's National Speakers Association. She has a BA in Psychology and Masters from UT in Organizational Development & Leadership. She is an executive coach with Center for Creative Leadership.

Fractured Teams from Broken Trust
Building the Path Back to Remarkable Teamwork

Scott Carley

FONDEST MEMORIES ARE ABOUT TEAMWORK

Some of my fondest memories and deepest disappointments are about teamwork and the exciting accomplishments we've achieved. One of those was as Area Director of BNI (Business Networking International). Bill and I managed 36 Chapters in central Texas that involved nearly 1100 members and generated over $36 million in referral revenue annually. It wasn't that way when we started! Yet through an incredible team, we were able to turn things around and get the attention of BNI's founder, Ivan Misner.

It's really invigorating to be involved in a team that works well together and gets things done. It's energizing to dream about the possibilities and imagine where we could go with an idea. I thrive on planning and strategizing our next move. When you get a group of people together who trust each other and feel the liberty to put their ideas out on the table without being ignored or shot down, you can really make incredible things happen! You cover one another's back and put your brains together to push through obstacles. It's amazing what group collaboration and group intelligence can accomplish!

We've produced phenomenal results despite the unbelievable odds against us. And then, together we've marched right up to the stage to proudly receive our trophies and awards. With huge smiles, the whole team posed for photo opportunities and then danced at the galas with the deep satisfaction that our team "pulled it off" and set a new benchmark for others to follow! Not exactly the Super Bowl, Masters or World Series... but just as good to us! Ahhhh...Teamwork!

My model for a phenomenal team can be found at Netflix: Danny Ocean's Eleven. Danny Ocean wanted to rob three casinos simultaneously that were owned by Terry Benedict, the man now dating his ex-wife, Tess. So there was more motive than just money. Danny contacted Reuben Tishkoff, a rival of Terry Benedict and he agreed to finance the heist.

Danny assembled an inner core and then an exclusive team of experts! They were a versatile group of highly specialized and committed criminals... or experts... who could pull off his crazy but grand idea to steal $160,000,000! There was no bickering. Everyone knew up front what the stakes were and the commitment required. Despite the odds, they employed their best skills and entertained us the whole way through! Step by step, scene by scene, they opened that impenetrable safe and pillaged Benedict's wealth. So cool to see them gather outside the Bellagio with their rewards, loot and small talk before riding off into the sunset! Clear roles. Clear risks. Clear rewards. Absolute mutual buy-in required. Now that's my idea of Teamwork!

When teamwork trust is remarkable, the flow of productivity is quick, the atmosphere is vivacious and the return is extraordinary!

MOST TEAMS ARE A MESS

Back in reality most teams are not like that. Most teams are a mess! They are fractured by broken trust, individualism and lack of vision. Not because they aren't in the movies with actors and writers, but because they have issues and splinters that sabotage their best efforts and intentions.

TEAMS ARE MADE UP OF INDIVIDUALS

"People inspire you or they drain you – pick them wisely."
— **Hans F. Hansen**

Teams are made up of individuals! Those team members may have open or underlying problems or disputes. When those sensitive areas are rubbed the wrong way, negative reactions can turn teamwork upside down in a flash. Drama queens can misread comments and melt into tears or anger. Exaggerators can be called out as liars, the office comedian can turn into a cultural showboat and a top selling champion can get his ego bruised and turn into a rude and ruthless hit man!

Huge problems can roam the office and flop down in a team meeting unexpectedly. Now the whole atmosphere of the meeting has gone south because there is an "elephant in the room" and nobody knows how to address it. Everyone is talking about it off site, texting about it to each other, but NOBODY is going to bring it up for a real discussion. It takes courage to have those hard conversations.

Suspicion and skepticism arising from a broken commitments or an outright lie by one or more team member can really shut down communication and productivity. When trust is fractured, the flow of productivity crumbles, the atmosphere is tense and the return is marginal.

Low morale is among the most common problems of fractured teams. Members shut down and lose enthusiasm. Involvement and production wane. Half-hearted efforts bring every aspect of teamwork to a miserable, dull decline. Low morale can either be the result of a direct trust fracture, an outright breach of integrity or the dismissal of a key team member. But low morale can also be the result of a lack of visionary leadership!

The main point is that a team is energized and becomes remarkable one player at a time.

FRACTURED TEAM CHARACTERS

Let me introduce you to a few Fractured Team Characters. Do any of these people sound familiar to you?

DRAMA QUEEN – DARLA

Never ask Darla, "How are you doing?" She will take your "off the cuff" remark as an invitation to vent her emotions and satisfy your curious interest with dramatic details that may suck you into her foaming rapids of DRAMA! She is never short on tragedy and is always looking for a listening ear. Darla can derail a team meeting and redirect its productive energies around her swirling calamities. Don't open that Pandora's box!

YES... most of the time people are significantly affected by their personal, domestic, health or financial issues. That's something to research before putting them in the rowboat with you! While we all have some level of issues to handle, it doesn't mean we have to be a Drama Queen.

DISHONEST DAN

Dan continuously presents a false narrative. If his lips are moving - you're NOT getting the full story. Most of the time his comments are just an exaggeration of the truth in one direction or another. But he has a reputation for outright dishonesty, too! That takes a huge hit on his Trust Credit Score. It especially does if his "stretching the truth" significantly affects the progress of the team or even the final outcome and rewards.

Rarely to his face, but often to the rest of the team, members will call out Dan as a "flat out liar!" Once his dishonesty is verified and the team has to swallow the ramifications, members will pull back and shift their confidence away from Dan. His word will never be taken at face value again.

Sometimes, Dan is the person who speaks "optimistically" about what he hopes to accomplish. His intentions are well meant, but he erodes trust in the group when he can't meet his own predictions. The backlash is loss of credibility. OUCH! It wasn't necessarily his intention or abject dishonesty; he just couldn't live up to his promises.

SHOWBOAT SAM ON A SOAP BOX

Sam is sanguine: enthusiastic, active and social. He is a comedian and a talker. And it's ALL about HIM or his Soap Box. He always has something to say, and it doesn't necessarily pertain to the point at hand. As a matter of fact, he is among the best to get the team off on a rabbit trail.

Sam has soap box topics. He has a "bee in his bonnet" and is going to use the team as his audience to vent his opinions and crank up the temperature. He has an agenda and his intentions get obvious quickly. Sam is only half aware how deeply he is offending some members on the team and alienating others from working beside him.

Unfortunately Sam rarely has any solutions. His poison is to identify all the problems, inconsistencies and wrong doings. And he is very good at it! Sam has a certification in pointing fingers and analyzing deficiencies as an armchair quarterback. But it's always "somebody else's" job to fix the problem.

Eventually the rest of the team starts to skirt social discussions or company policies because they know Sam will start off on one of his "rants" and who knows where it will go and how it will end.

MISSING MARTHA

Where is Martha? We have this meeting every third Monday and she is never here! What is up with her? Martha decided to do a site visit today... because she hasn't done her homework for this committee. Yep...the dog ate her homework, so Martha is absent. Again!

She is always calling in "sick" or "waiting on a home delivery. If she can find a reason to leave the office for a site visit, then she can run a bunch of personal errands and then head home early. It's not supposed to be noticeable because it's only for half a day here and there, but HR got a tip and has started monitoring her attendance.

What is the deal with Martha? Why is she so unreliable on attendance? She has been with us for nearly 20 years and has become infected with entitlement. She is on salary and doesn't have to put in 40 hours. "Seriously, who does that anymore?" Attending her committee meetings or participating in her team roles is at the bottom of her list. Martha doesn't have buy-in to her team and their projects. Why is she here? Because she was transferred over from another department having the same issues with keeping her engaged. HR is on to her now. Two more infractions and she will be escorted from the building.

TOP GUN TOM

This guy is a winner! Tom is top salesman quarter after quarter. He can close deals and make sales. There is no telling how much revenue he has created for the company. But he knows it! While his team cannot deny his track record, neither can they deny his arrogance and rude behavior in the group.

NOBODY wants to work with Tom! He sees everything as a personal challenge. If he sniffs out any competition in a team meeting, he goes into "topping your story" mode. His insecurities are clear to everyone but him and his over compensation just makes the team roll their eyes. People get tired of patting him on the shoulder and stoking his ego.

Tom doesn't share his secrets or tactics. Anything you get is pried from his white knuckles. His attitude and behavior send strong signals of distrust and individualism. He is only a team player because he feels like THEY need him, not the other way around. But everyone else knows the truth; what makes Tom so successful is all the work the team does to support and deliver for him. Customer support works long hours to make good on all of Tom's promises. But when he gets too far out there, the team no longer wants to be his catch person.

HAS-BEEN HENRIETTA

Henrietta is all about the past. She cannot get her eyes off her rear view mirror. It looks good back there! And as time goes by, the past looks better and better. Actually the facts from the past get a little distorted in her advantage, too. Henrietta looks better and better in her version of those successes. "Five years ago at my old company, we snapped this thing together under budget and ahead of schedule!"

Could somebody please bring Henrietta into the present? Vernacular has changed.

Technology has significantly advanced. Most of the software programs you are referring to are no longer supported. Storage is now on the Cloud; you will be given an access code. We don't use cables anymore; it's all blue tooth. Nobody is coming in for a all day seminar; we will be training remote around the country with video screen share. Though the team respects and appreciates Henrietta's history of experience and success, they need her to come up to speed and get competent with the present.

Millennials are not just in the workforce but they are also decision makers. Every metropolitan city is cosmopolitan and their cultures have to be integrated into how we work and our vocabulary adjusted. Henrietta resists new ways of doing things. Her natural peripheral vision is toward the past, not the present or future. While patient for a while, now it is becoming obvious to the team that she is stagnant; has stopped growing intellectually and socially. The team is questioning her capabilities and coming up with a low credit score.

YOU HAVE A TRUST CREDIT SCORE

Consciously or not, teams evaluate one another on a constant basis. It's not on paper or necessarily intentional; but it's happening. We rate one another all the time and then based on our findings, cooperate or resist.

The reality is each member on the team has a Trust Credit Score in at least four areas:

- Intent – The motives behind their actions and what they say or imply

- Integrity – The perception of their character, values and morals

- Capabilities – Do they have the qualifications and skill set?

- Results – Can they really get the job done under budget and ahead of schedule?

Every day or every week your TCS moves up or down the scale with the rest of the team. Their trust in you is verified and strengthened or it slides off and doubt and suspicion begins to rise. Our words, but more importantly our behavior fuels our Teamwork Trust Credit Score.

Darla, Dan, Sam, Martha, Tom, Henrietta and all the other team members are either sabotaging their Trust Credit Scores or repairing them. Finally there is a way to repair broken or damaged trust through conscious behaviors. WOW...what a relief!

BROKEN TRUST LEADS TO FRACTURED TEAMS

These characters help us understand the main Fractures of Teamwork. When trust is remarkable, the flow of productivity is quick, the atmosphere is vivacious and the return is extraordinary. But when teamwork is fractured and trust is broken, the flow of productivity crumbles, the atmosphere is tense and the return is marginal. Teams shut down. They quit performing. Members lose heart while others outright revolt. Trust in individual member's intentions, integrity, skills and getting the job done either fractures or encourages remarkable teamwork.

FIVE FRACTURES OF TEAMWORK

The first thing that has to happen is recognizing the most common areas of a fractured team. If these things are present, they are symptoms of a much deeper issue. Until they are addressed, a team cannot repair itself and get back on track. Often it's uncomfortable and risky. But the rewards are remarkable.

Here are the Five Fractures of Teamwork

1. Avoiding Hard Conversations

2. Suspicions and Skepticism

3. Dissents and Non-Conformism

4. Evasiveness and Ambiguity

5. Mediocrity and Status Addiction

Jeanette's alarm goes off at 6:30 and she fumbles around to find the snooze. It's her training week and she is not motivated to get up and get going. A half hour later she is applying her makeup and decides to let it slide today. It's going to be a long morning with Showboat Sam. OMG he is so into himself.

Rush hour is normal so getting to work won't be a pinch. Jeanette set up the room on Friday with all the computers in place and connected to their server. Someone else is covering the student workbooks. She can go in and get her coffee before everyone gets there.

Buzz buzz. Martha's voice comes on line as she quickly asks Jeanette if she's "there" yet. "Nope, I'm on my way, but I'm 20 minutes out. What's up?" "Oh Jeanette… I'm waiting on a delivery here at the house from FedEx that requires a signature. I can't make it in until after 10:30. Can you finish up the student book? It just needs the cover and to be stapled? Hey I'll owe you one, girl!"

Jeanette says, "Sure...no problem, Martha." But inside she is steaming! It's almost 8:00 and class starts at 8:30. She is still 20 minutes away. OMG...Martha did it again! Three out of four Monday training sessions, she has called in late. I'm sure it has nothing to do with their weekend trips to Corpus! This is the last time! Next week, the students will get their guides when Martha gets to work. Jeanette is resolved to not cover for her again.

Jeanette rushes into the building, puts her stuff down and starts looking for Martha's "almost finished" workbooks. Just then Sam come around the corner with a big smirk and full of excitement! "Oh Jeanette... have I got a hot story for class today!" OMG...please not another social injustice to fuel Sam's nonstop rants! It's like he lives for the moment when he can accost his classes with the evils of social injustice and special interest group rights that have been violated in the latest newscast. It's going to be a long day. Jeanette just wants to get her part done, finish the day and go home.

Right after Jeanette starts the class, but before she introduces Sam, Monique (their department supervisor) slides into the training room and takes a back seat. She smiles at Jeanette as she pulls out her notepad. It's the first time in months that Monique has actually come in for a class audit. Once Sam is introduced and turned lose to begin his soapbox rant, Jeanette sits beside Monique and welcomes her to the class. Monique quietly whispers, "HR suggested I sit in today and see what's going on.

Could it be that Monique is actually going to address our team fractures by having a hard conversation with Martha and then Sam?

Scott Carley is described as a "maverick catalyst," specializing in goal setting, priority management, and repairing fractured teams. As a business coach, he travels the country speaking at conferences and for CEO VISTAGE masterminds and executive teams. He believes in the power of relationship currency, and has a passion to help professionals overcome their obstacles and reach their BIG goals! Scott spent the first 25 years of his career as a Pastor and a Church Growth Consultant traveling to over 300 cities. He is an award winning Managing Area Director for BNI (Business Networking International), taking his 45 chapters to the top 2% internationally in growth, retention and referral revenue ($36 million annually). As a speaker/trainer, Scott captures the imagination of his audiences with his quick humor and contagious energy. He has a unique ability to cut through the "stuff" and get to the heart of productivity. Contact him at Scott@ScottCarley.com.

Hard Earned Lessons

Floyd McLendon, Jr.

Thirty years ago, I was a shy, inner city, African-American, young man embarking on a journey of integrity, character, mental fortitude, physical transformation, and accountability. It is the required crucible for all young men to becoming a man of substance and a contribution to society. I flunked out of college, pursued a professional basketball career, became a U.S. Navy SEAL, fully recovered from severe physical trauma, served 25 years in the military, became a highly-inspirational public speaker, and have positioned myself to publicly serve in the legislative and/or executive branch. But getting to this point required life experience filled with lessons... Hard Earned Lessons.

During my eighth grade graduation I was told by my father, "You are now a young man and do not have to take mess from anyone!" Up until that point in my life, I had been considered an easy target because of my smaller body frame and easy-going nature. I grew up in a generation where we fought with our hands. I had lost my fair share of fights, but lived to talk about it the next day. This stands in stark contrast to the environment that seems to have swallowed many of our inner cities today. This particular day, I absorbed my father's words and decided to never lose a physical altercation or back away from a challenge. To this day, I never have. My father's words, on that occasion, were my first insight into the power of the mind.

Two months into my high school freshman year, while waiting for first period to start, an upperclassman began bullying my best friend. The upperclassman's aggression towards my best friend rubbed me the wrong way. I came to his defense. Things escalated, the upperclassman suffered a broken nose, and I received a one-week suspension from school. My parents were upset and grounded me for an additional week. I believed I accurately followed the advice of my father — taking no mess from anyone. He told me later that I had failed to use good judgment by resorting to fighting, which should have been the last option. I became rebellious. I felt wronged. I struggled to make sense of the apparent dichotomy.

Before my suspension, I earned "A's" in all of my classes and was a model student. I developed an attitude and lost interest in maintaining exceptional grades. My history teacher was concerned over the sudden change in my attitude and literally cried, voicing to me her concern over how rapidly my grades had deteriorated. I will always remember her caring spirit and how it changed my perspective on teachers' commitment to their profession. Teachers really do make a significant, positive impact. Eventually, I bounced back, earning good grades, but it took my GPA half a year to recover.

During my sophomore year I began to excel at playing basketball. I had maintained a love for the sport since sixth grade and still remember the summer between seventh and eighth grade when I grew three inches. The next summer, between eighth grade and high school, I grew another three inches. After my freshman year, I attended the Michael Jordan Basketball Camp. All of this led to a positive transformation, mentally and physically, and even though I knew I would not be able to play high school basketball, based on my family's faith, I still wanted to excel at the highest possible level. I grew up as a 7th Day Adventist, which included worship from Friday to Saturday evening during which time "worldly" interests were not permitted, including television, radio, school events, etc. Most of the games for high school sports occurred on Friday or Saturday and none of the coaches would allow me to partially participate. In my youthful mind, I wanted to play professional basketball, and realized I would have to find an alternative route towards this endeavor given the imposed limitations of my parents' faith.

At age 14, I tried out for my church's basketball team. Though the age requirement was 16, it was overlooked because of my skill level. I routinely played against men seven to ten years older and my development grew exponentially. Whenever I did play against my peers, my confidence and higher skill level was evident. After serious coaxing from multiple players in the church, my father agreed to allow me to try out for my school's basketball team.

The basketball season had already started, but the coach allowed a late tryout. My first day of tryouts, on a Monday, I made the team. When I got home, my father expressed his reservations about allowing me to play and, in less than a week, he was beginning to change his mind. However, he said I was old enough to decide and would leave the choice up to me. Tuesday night, I attended a home game, sat on the bench and just observed. Wednesday, I had a good practice. I was told I would receive my practice and game uniforms early the next day and that I would play in Friday's game. Also, I met the varsity coach who indicated he was considering bringing me up to the varsity team. When I got home that evening, my father had changed his mind and the decision to play on the team was revoked. I was devastated. I broke down and cried. This was a very difficult lesson in integrity and trust. Through my father's shortcomings, I learned to be a man of my word and someone people could trust.

Spring of 1991, I graduated high school and started my freshman year at the University of Illinois, Champaign-Urbana, with plans to focus on Computer Engineering. The only thing I knew about Computer Engineering was it sounded impressive. I remained passionate about basketball, but valued my parents' and mentors' advice: wait until sophomore year so—during freshman year—I could focus on my studies. I knew my parents and mentors meant well, but in retrospect, I should have ignored their advice. Like many young adults away from parent's scrutiny for the first time, I fell short of my academic goals. I never took my classes seriously and did more socializing than studying. Truthfully, I went to college to get away from home and my grades were a direct reflection. Freshman year, had I tried out for the team, I would have earned the grades to remain eligible and been successful with the pursuit of a degree. After first semester, I was put on academic probation. After second semester, I became academically ineligible for the Fall of 1992. Rightfully earned, my parents decided to not financially support my college education. That experience taught me that, ultimately, the decision is mine. Be wise in communicating with confidants and value their opinion, but I am solely responsible and held accountable for the results.

Summer of 1992, I enlisted into the United States Naval Reserve. My plan was to have the Navy pay for my education while I served one weekend a month and two weeks a year. In August of 1992, I graduated from Navy Boot Camp in Orlando, FL. When I returned home, I petitioned the University of Illinois for reinstatement for the Spring semester. The GI Bill, financial aid, student loans, and student work program were now the source of my educational income. My parents were officially out of the academic financial equation, but they felt the need to continue managing my life. I grew increasingly discouraged with attending college and I decided to put my education on hold until I was ready and able to completely support myself.

Summer of 1993, I enlisted for active duty in the U.S. Navy. I chose to be an Electronic Technician because I wanted a profession I could use following my military career. Ironically, I had been trying to get away from school and ended up spending the next two years in specialized classes that were required for my Navy rating. I was in school again. I graduated from Electronic Technician 'A' School in February 1995 and checked into my first command, the USS Kalamazoo (AOR- 6). The Kalamazoo was a replenishment oiler that provided fuel, food, and supplies to other naval vessels. My primary responsibilities involved maintaining our radar and satellite communications. My secondary responsibilities ranged from polishing brass, cleaning toilets, standing four-six hour watches, to manning the refueling stations during underway refueling. The latter could be brutal at times because, regardless of the weather, we stuck to the schedule. One particular winter day we were underway, refueling another ship. Imagine a giant garden hose extending from one ship to another, transferring hundreds of gallons of fuel. Both ships must travel side-by-side, same speed, same bearing, so the connected hose does not unexpectedly break away.

This particular day, the sea state was rough and the temperature was in the 20s. The water in between the ships was very choppy, which created big waves that splashed onto the deck where we were working. The cold, wet conditions forced our crew to swap out personnel every fifteen minutes because of the fear of hypothermia. After my 15-minute shift I would go to my sleeping quarters, change into another set of dry layers, grab some hot chocolate, and head back out to my station to relieve the previous sailor. Where most were upset and complaining about the conditions, I was excited, and relished in the adverse weather conditions. The danger of possibly being swept off the deck into the ocean was oddly exhilarating. Like the fight in high school which developed my moral being, the subversion by my father that led to being a man of my word, and my failures at college which forced taking charge of my life, this too became a day I would always remember in defining the man I was becoming.

In 1996, I transferred to the USS John F. Kennedy (CV-67), an aircraft carrier stationed in Mayport, FL. I still had dreams of playing professional basketball and set my mind to making the All Navy Basketball Team, then the All Armed Forces Basketball Team. Eventually I hoped to get exposure overseas, drafted by a foreign country, then drafted by the NBA. I was 23 years old and believed it was possible. At the All Navy Tryouts in 1997, unbeknownst to me, I suffered an Achilles tendon injury to my right leg. For one week, I played on a partially torn Achilles tendon before I was cut from the team. Yet, another moment of adversity to contend with, learn from, and re-evaluate the direction of my life. The following year, All Navy Tryouts were held at my base in Mayport, FL. I made the team as a shooting guard, but was disappointed because I was not selected as one of the starting five. I was the best player on the team at that position. This was the first time with open eyes I saw how politics played into everyday situations.

Half of the players selected for the team had played the year before. They already had established amicable relationships with the coaching staff, most notably the head coach. During that year's Armed Forces tournament, my playing time was minimal. We won the bronze medal and I was left with a bad taste in my mouth. I felt we could have placed higher had the coach utilized me more. I decided that if the same head coach was present the following season, I would not continue playing for All Navy.

In 1999, I transferred to Naval Air Station Patuxent River, MD. Coincidentally, that July, the All Armed Forces Basketball Team came to Patuxent River to prepare for the European Trials. The All Navy head coach was an assistant coach for All Armed Forces and he asked if I was going to try out for All Navy that year. I politely declined. My focus had changed. I had two years left on my enlistment and I wanted to take advantage of shore duty by completing as much college as possible. Little did I know another path was about to present itself.

One of my coworkers had expressed an interest in the U.S. Navy SEALs. He was about to start training to prepare for their school, Basic Underwater Demolition/SEAL (BUD/S). One of my life goals was to learn how to swim proficiently, so I agreed to train with him. The training began to grow on me and the more I dedicated my time and effort, the more I wanted to pursue going to BUD/S. My co-worker did not qualify for the program, but I stuck with the training and prepared myself for my own BUD/S Physical Screening Test (PST).

Three months later, I was comfortable enough in the water to learn the required swim stroke for the BUD/S PST, the Combat Side Stroke (CSS). Up until that point, I would do my best imitation of a freestyle stroke and swim the distance dictated by my training plan. I completely immersed myself into training and researched everything I could find that pertained to the profession of a U.S. Navy SEAL. Six months into my training, I took an official BUD/S PST to be considered for selection to BUD/S. I barely passed the swim. Considering that six months earlier I could not swim, I thought I did very well. I screened positive for the program and was given orders to BUD/S for the following year, which fortunately allowed me to continue strengthening my body and acclimating to the water. In March 2002, I moved to San Diego, CA and checked into BUD/S.

In November 2002, I voluntarily removed myself from training. I quit! During the infamous Hell Week, I developed a gastrointestinal virus. I lost 30 pounds over a three-month period and went from 190 lbs. to 160 lbs. My performance significantly dropped off and my body began to lock-up and shut down. Completing Hell Week was not my concern, rather it was how much permanent damage I would sustain when I did. In the moment, it was a very difficult decision, but remains one I look back on to this day. I had made the right one. I was beginning to identify what true physical limitations felt like and trust my decision-making process. Once I was removed from training, my body was able to repair itself. The combination of mental and physical training stressors, the lack of rest and recovery, had inhibited my body from healing. Had I decided to continue training, I believe I would have inflicted permanent damage to my body and been medically dropped. My desire to become a U.S. Navy SEAL had not been assuaged and I knew I would return to BUD/S.

In February 2003, I transferred to the USS Cleveland (LPD-7). Upon arriving at this new command, I informed my leadership of my desires to return to BUD/S. I was committed to giving the Cleveland two years of enthusiastic, hard work, but asked for their support when I re-submitted my request to go back to BUD/S. They agreed. To continue improving in my water skills, I volunteered to be a Search and Rescue Swimmer for the ship, which required going to Search and Rescue Swimmer School (SRSS). I graduated at the top of my class, receiving the Honor Man Award. The water training in SRSS boosted my confidence and I became very comfortable in the water. I felt aquatically prepared for my future ambition. My opportunity of returning to BUD/S came nine months sooner than I expected. My command supported me and I was fortunate I had not stopped preparing. I felt blessed that life had afforded me an opportunity to prove myself, again.

The rigors of training were still the same, monumental. I found it to be more physically challenging than what I remembered, due in no small part to the fact that I was now 31 years old. Toward the end of some weeks, I was at my physical limit and barely held it together. Going through this process, day after day, week after week, for a year-and-a-half, physically tore my body to pieces. By the time I graduated from BUD/S, my back, knees, and shoulders were a wreck.

In December 2005, almost six years after deciding to become a U.S. Navy SEAL, it became a reality. I had earned the Special Warfare Insignia; known casually within the community as the "Trident." Before checking into my first SEAL command, I attended a few skill-specific schools. This allowed time for my mind and body to rest and recover. I believe during the recovery process from severe trauma, the human body grows into a stronger version. During that time, I added 10 pounds to my slim frame and experienced a greater, mental transformation.

Life is about lessons and being able to positively apply those lessons to future decisions. Twelve years later, five times forward deployed, and four years as a High-Risk Naval Special Warfare (NSW) Instructor supporting this great country's ideals and policies, I often reflect on these first, important lessons. Despite the many challenges I faced growing-up, which pale in comparison to the struggles others have endured, BUD/S taught me to trust in my preparation, trust in my teammates and instructors, and trust in my training.

Looking back, though, I laugh! In retrospect, earning my Trident was merely the beginning. Back in those moments, I felt that life's challenges were HUGE...not realizing everything I endured was laying the foundation to successfully navigate to greater accomplishments. The challenges have forged a passionate, internal desire and commitment to serve for causes greater than my own. Now, I understand. My blueprints have been drawn to prevail over adversity. There are many, more challenges in the future, on the road to becoming a prominent for our great nation. I am prepared to learn the Hard Earned Lessons. *And, I will not lose sleep over the opinions of sheep.*

◇◇

Floyd McLendon Jr. is a native of the south-side of Chicago, Illinois. For 25 years, he honorably served in the greatest, naval military in the world, 15 years as a U.S. Navy SEAL. The last seven years of his military career, in addition to maintaining operational readiness, Floyd was a motivational speaker for the Naval Special Warfare (NSW) community. He travelled nationwide to educate high schools, colleges, and community centers on the diversity NSW had to offer and shared the mental toughness techniques used to achieve mission success. He forward deployed five times, with presence in 24 countries over five continents. Floyd, now, is an experienced and highly inspirational speaker with a purpose to positively affect people's lives. He is passionate about the development, execution, and evaluation of initiatives that inspire those who seek improvement professionally, socially, mentally, and/or physically.

Control Your Brain, Enjoy Your Life

Helene Segura, MA Ed, CPO®

Jenna told herself for the umpteenth day in a row, "You got nothing done today!"

She had a habit of beating herself up over not achieving her goals. She was driving herself into the ground — then feeling down and out — because she never felt like she was successful. The more she wallowed in self-disappointment, the less she was able to focus.

The art of focus is a dying one. And that's why so many people feel like they are spinning their wheels. They're in such a hurry to get everything done that they stumble, make mistakes, forget things or get sidetracked and, ultimately, get nothing done — or at least very little.

If you're like Jenna and want to better manage your time so that you can accomplish your goals, you must begin by paying attention to what's going on in your mind.

When clients first meet me, they're super stressed and want to learn immediate productivity hacks — the best task app to download, the best calendar to use…. What they soon learn as we dive into the session is that the most creative hacks in the world won't do a lick of good if your mind isn't thinking clearly. After all, it's your brain that decides what goes on the calendar and whether or not you'll work on anything in that task app. It's your brain that decides whether you're going to procrastinate or move forward.

The more you control your mind and pay attention to what's in front of you, the more productive you'll be. And when you can harness your time and improve your productivity, that will allow you to enjoy life on your terms.

Here are seven ways to help you accomplish this:

◊ 1 Value your mind. ◊

Jenna and I were discussing in her office all of the different tasks that were pulling her brain away from what she does best — working billable client hours. Her gift of developing training curriculum helps her clients, her clients are happy, and she generates revenue, which makes her bank account and household happy.

But she has more "task hours" on her calendar than billable hours because she won't farm out some of the work that needs to get done. Part of it is because she's afraid of letting someone else do the work. The other part is the expense — she doesn't want to shell out money for what she is capable of doing.

Suddenly, we were interrupted by a knock on the office door. A tree-trimming crew was cruising the area looking for jobs. She asked how much it would be for them to trim every tree on the lot. She did not bat an eyelash when they said $2800, and she immediately retrieved her checkbook.

She did not know them or their reputation or whether or not they even knew what they were doing. But she hired them on the spot.

When we got back into her office, we continued our chat.

How did it feel to get that task off your plate? I asked her.

"Great!" exclaimed she.

Why did you decide to delegate that task?

"Well, can you see me hanging off a ladder with a chainsaw? I'd probably chop off one of my arms! Besides being dangerous, I have no business using my time for that."

I see you value your life and limb.

"Ha! Pun intended?"

I see you value your time when it comes to delegating tasks that require strenuous physical output or sweating.

"Yeah! Who wants to do that dirty stuff?"

Do you value your mind the same way?

Silence.

We tend to take what's in our brains for granted. We need to put a value on our intellect and our mental gifts. Delegate your chainsaw tasks so you can use your genius for more important objectives — like growing your business or career and earning a comfortable living.

When you value your mind, you'll understand how much power you have in harnessing your time.

◇ 2 DECIDE IF YOU'RE THE PENCIL LEAD OR THE ERASER. ◇

Every day is exciting for me because I get to coach an individual or group on organizing and productivity and help them curb the stress that they're under. Sometimes, though, I get a request to return to my past life as a teacher, and each time I learn something new from observing the students.

For five years in a row, I was requested to conduct a workshop series at a particular high school with students who had been removed from their standard classroom environments. They'd been invited to leave their home campuses for a variety of reasons such as misbehavior, truancy or arrests. The choices and mistakes they'd made had caused them to fall behind in their credits by one year or more. My job was to get them focused for their exit exams and help them with decision-making skills along the way. In a nutshell, I tried to rewire how their brains think and plan for life so they could become productive citizens.

We had the same routine at the beginning of each one of my sessions. The students picked up their activity packets and borrowed a pencil and highlighter to use for the class period. It struck me one day when I watched how the students chose their pencils that their choices reflected who they are. Those who chose their pencils based on the sharpness of the writing tip were the same students who were working hard to make changes in their lives and get back on track. The students who chose their pencils based on the condition of the eraser were the same students who were fumbling aimlessly in life. They were already planning to make mistakes and erase the mess. Their counterparts, on the other hand, chose based on the tool they needed to complete their work; if they wound up needing an eraser later, they knew where to get one.

The attitude you have in your approach to tasks and projects will determine your success.

If you start every day prepping for your tasks and telling yourself you will complete them, then you will. But if you start every day with the expectation that you won't meet the standards, well, you'll do just that. Your thoughts determine your success.

So, how will you choose your pencil: by the sharpness of the tip or the size of the eraser?

◊ 3 TASTE YOUR FOOD. ◊

Do you ever take the time to taste your food?

Do you allow the aroma of what you're about to taste waft into your nostrils?

Do you then imagine what the taste will be like?

Do you let each bite slowly melt in your mouth?

Do you pause after you swallow your food and try to determine what the ingredients are?

If your answer is no, you're not alone. Hundreds of thousands of people each day shovel food into their mouths without a second thought. They consume food because they know that they need to in order to survive, but they don't take the time to choose something good for their bodies, nor savor what they're eating.

This is what happens to a lot of busy professionals. They get behind in what they think they should be doing and jump on a merry-go-round in overdrive. They go, go, go — spinning their wheels all day long, but rarely having anything to show for it at the end of the day.

If you feel like this, it's time to take a step back.

What nutrients does your business or career truly need in order to grow?

What flavors of projects would you like to pursue because they'll make you happy or advance your career or both?

What will your meal plan be for the next week?

If you want to be more productive, start to think like a foodie. Take your time. Experience and examine your moments. When you do this, your brain will make better decisions about how you use your time, which will lead you down the road to success and happiness.

◊ 4 DEFINE WHAT SIMPLICITY MEANS TO YOU. ◊

I was recently pondering simplicity after trying to upgrade to the latest home theater gadget and having everything go horribly wrong. I cursed all gadgets and components and blamed them for complicating my life. I continued my lamenting until a few days later when I blew out a tire during the middle of a monsoon and was able to not only get my tire fixed but make it to my client appointment on time all because of a gadget — my smartphone's internet service allowed me to Google the nearest tire shop and get help.

I quit my demonizing of technology and reminded myself that simplicity goes deeper than my relationship with gadgets. It's directly connected to my belief in streamlining processes and living efficiently. My analysis concluded that the times when I wished that my life was simpler were the times when I realized that a) I'm throwing a tantrum because I didn't get my way or b) I have too many commitments on my plate. I generally avoid the latter because I go through the same reflection exercise that I tell my clients to do at the end of each week or month. It's a time when I readjust and jettison a project or two in order to return to simpler times. In the case of my gadget (ahem) meltdown, I sheepishly admit that my problem was the former — which is also easy enough to fix.

My solution to easing my stress levels is based on my definition of simpler. Your solution will be based on your definition. What causes you to say, "I wish my life was simpler"?

Do you say that when you're drop dead tired from running around like a chicken with its head cut off — all day, every day?

Do you say that when you look around your home and don't even know where to begin an organizing project because there's entirely too much stuff?

Do you say that when you're sitting at a weekly lunch engagement surrounded by people you don't like?

Do you say that after you realize that you've complicated a process that should be much simpler?

Do you say that when you look around at all of your unfinished projects?

Why do you make that wish?

When you figure out your answer, you'll figure out how to indeed make your life simpler, which will help your brain make better decisions about how you use your time.

◊ 5 Confront the more difficult. ◊

One afternoon, Jenna shared with me, "I've noticed this tendency. When I get to a filing or record keeping task that is just a little more difficult than usual, I flee! I want to leave the scene. Maybe I tell myself I need a snack for energy to go on, or decide I need to check on something in a different area of the office. The truth is, I am fleeing. I get up, I get distracted, I forget the problem I had encountered — with no resolution. What tricks do you use to get back to work?"

I responded, *Great job realizing that this is happening! Have you considered preparing a "what-I-can-do-when-I-feel-the-flee-coming-on list" so that you can nip this avoidance habit in the bud? For example, an idea to add to your list is to stop and ask yourself, 'How will delaying this task benefit me?'*

Because overcoming the desire to flee requires the logical part of your brain to outsmart the emotional part of your brain, this means that you'll be playing mind games with yourself. And this means that different solutions will work in different moments — the same solution won't work 100% of the time. That's why I recommend that you keep the aforementioned list of ideas of what you can do when you feel this urge coming on. Post the list in your work area. When the urge hits, pull one of the solutions from the list to help you move forward.

By confronting your challenges head on, you'll gain confidence in your decision-making skills and your power to accomplish what you perceive to be difficult tasks. With this confidence, you'll make even better decisions about how you use your time.

◊ 6 Change your disasters to inconveniences. ◊

When Jenna and I were determining which productivity tools would be best for her situation, she suddenly blurted out, "Are all of your clients in turmoil?!?"

She'd been exasperated since the moment I'd walked in. There was upheaval at work. Her employer was going through yet another "reorganization" to improve processes and cut expenses, but the prior "reorg" had never been successfully completed. The physical space in her home was weighing her down as well. Her office had become a dumping ground, so she'd begun working in the living room. The living room, after a while, was no longer the living room since it was full of work material. One dilemma after another kept cropping up at work and at home. She was tired of dealing with all of the chaos. She wanted some comfort - to know that she wasn't alone, that she wasn't the only one who had a life like this.

Hence, her question, "Are all of your clients in turmoil?!?"

My answer:

When our life at work feels out of balance, we tend to go downhill and not use our productivity tools, so we become less efficient. Our frustration leads to muddied waters in the brain, which leads to sub-par decision-making. This brain constipation at work often spills over into our personal life. We've got thoughts and ideas swirling around in our heads, trying to break free, but nothing will come out. This blockage causes us to also make less than stellar decisions outside of work.

When we make a series of less than optimal decisions, it starts to multiply our overwhelm. When our overwhelm builds up, we think that any less-than-perfect happening is a disaster. Our out-of-control spin intensifies, and we think the world is against us.

When we get back into balance, we still have the same types of issues and the same less-than-perfect happenings, but because we're thinking clearly and feeling calm, we don't see those situations as chaos or disaster. Instead, we see them simply as inconveniences that we need to deal with as a part of life. The sooner we decide to take back control of our work and home lives, the sooner the chaos will leave.

So to answer your question, most of my clients think they're in turmoil. But as we get them back in balance, they do not allow said turmoil to enter their lives as often.

"Damn," said she. "That is so true. Let's get me some balance!"

When you recalibrate your perspective, you'll regain the balance in your brain, which will lead to better decision-making about how you use your time.

◊ 7 CELEBRATE THE LITTLE THINGS IN LIFE. ◊

One sunny afternoon, I arrived at Jenna's house for a home office session. Her kids knew me quite well, so they were never shy about running up to me and saying hello, even when Mommy wasn't yet in the room. On this particular occasion, I was not only greeted, but I was also given an exciting news bulletin by the three- and four-year-old children:

3 y.o.: "I ate a marshmallow."

4 y.o.: "Because she went poo poo!"

3 y.o.: "Yeah! I went poo poo!"

We raised our arms in the air and jumped up and down and celebrated that she went poo poo!

When's the last time you celebrated a seemingly minor accomplishment?

Heck, when's the last time you celebrated *anything* you've accomplished?

One of the practices that I encourage my clients to implement is that of reflecting with power at the end of each day. Too many times when we reflect, we start off by thinking about all of the things that we didn't get done...all of the tasks that we still have left to do. That's no fun! It's really discouraging, which de-motivates us and slows down any momentum we're trying to build up.

Instead, reflect with power. Start your reflection by recalling everything that you have gotten done — no matter how small you think it might be. You got out of bed. High five! You got dressed. Yeah, baby! You checked two items off your to-do list. Happy dance! You even remembered to bring in the reusable bags when you went to the grocery store. Score! Give yourself credit for the big and little things in life that you complete. If you focus on the positive and enjoy the little things in life, your brain will operate with more clarity, which will help you better harness your time.

As you work on improving your time management, you'll find — as Jenna did — that you have more time to focus on being intentional. As you focus on being intentional, you'll find that you are more successful with your time management techniques.

Out of all the productivity tools in the world, the most important one is your brain — because it's the source of all the decisions you make. Time management is truly all about mind management. Your brain is the cause of your failures. It is also the key to your successes.

If you want to improve your time management so that you can lower your stress levels, start with your mind. Control your brain. Harness your time. Enjoy your life.

◇◇◇

Do you want to wake up 10 years from now and lament, "I wish I'd lived a little more instead of work around the clock"? Helene Segura doesn't want to either. That's why she tells her time what to do—and teaches busy professionals how to do the same by slaying lost time. The author of two Amazon best-selling books, Helene has been the featured productivity expert in more than 150 media interviews. During her time management keynotes and workshops, she shares her mind-bending framework for decreasing interruptions, distractions and procrastination so that companies can spend more time generating revenue. On weekends, Helene can be found experimenting with recipes or sneaking adult beverages onto the lawn bowling court. For details about her third book, The Inefficiency Assassin: Time Management Tactics for Working Smarter, Not Longer *(New World Library) and to download a complimentary* Productivity Kickstarter Kit, *visit www.TimeManagementRevolution.com.*

Confidence

Jack Allen

Bear and I met on the Internet. I was piddling around on social media, and one of those "you should know this person" lines appeared with a face, a name, and an interesting caption about my old college fraternity. We connected and I received a very nice message from this guy asking if we could talk privately about a problem he was facing—he needed to talk to "someone with some wisdom."

Who could refuse a request like that? I had no idea how much this simple connection would lead to an incredible experience.

By his photographs and posts, the young man was a burly, friendly man. My immediate impression was that he is kind of a big teddy bear, and sure enough, he told me that his college nickname was "Bear" and that he was 6'2" and 300 pounds!

He told me that he had been at his job a year and his boss didn't like him. He described a toxic work atmosphere where people stole credit for ideas, gossiped, and played office politics. Employees routinely manipulated management with fake reports and claims. After ten minutes, I wanted to quit, and I didn't even work there!

I tell prospective clients to bring me a clear problem, we will at least start solving it within 20 minutes at no charge. Detoxing a work environment takes longer.

I glanced at the clock and saw that several minutes had evaporated. For a moment, I feared I'd over-promised. But belief is the stuff of progress: I believed we could make progress, and I took the risk of telling Bear: "We're going to solve this thing. It sounds like you want a promotion but do not believe you'll get one, is that it?"

Yes.

"And you believe the reason you will not get the promotion is the toxic work environment."

Yes, that's it. Should I find a new job? I've only been here a year and I don't want to look like a job hopper. These people are impossible though. You cannot believe the stupid &%$! I have to put up with. This might ruin my career. Why didn't I stay at my old job? My girlfriend is right, I should've stayed at [old company].

This went on for another full minute until I had to break in: "Bear, we're running low on time, so I will have to be blunt. You're right. You will not get the promotion. In fact, you'll probably get fired from this job."

What?

"Unless you regain your confidence."

In what?

"In you."

Okay, my confidence is low, but I know I can do the job. I know I can succeed here.

"You just told me three things that compete with each other. Only one of those can be true. Which one do you believe?"

Silence.

Except for the sound of the ticking clock. I really want to help this guy without rescheduling. Two-minute warning.

Finally, Bear said, "Okay. I need confidence. I guess I knew it but it seems like it's self-defeating to admit. What do I do?"

I am pleased to tell you that moment was a significant breakthrough. Within one month, he discovered beliefs that blocked his confidence. During the second month, he made friends at work and discovered a new revenue stream for his company. During the third month, Bear found yet another revenue stream, and was asked to lunch by his boss.

Bear went to lunch prepared to ask for a five percent raise. His boss would not let him talk until he had offered a promotion and a fifteen percent raise.

Oh, and he found a new, confidence building girlfriend and lost twenty-three pounds. All because he regained his confidence.

This brief piece is your author's way of helping you find your confidence, build upon it, and use it to achieve your dreams. I'll talk about confidence from two angles: that of an emerging talent—someone who wants to find the good life—and from the other direction, established talent—someone who wants to continue to have a good life.

Emerging Talent

You're newer in a career or company. Maybe you're straight out of school. Maybe you're coming into your first management level job. You know you have skills or you wouldn't have gotten this far. You have a little bit of confidence that you can take the next level but you struggle keeping up with the more experience people; you find yourself intimidated. You struggle to know where your career is headed. You lack a clear sense of what you want in life.

Can you find out what your boss thinks is a win? If you don't understand that, you likely do things that your supervisor does not care about. You might spend a lot of time on the wrong things and that further degrades your confidence.

My emerging clients tell me that college did not prepare them well for the workplace. There is a tremendous lack of confidence when one feels under-prepared for something so crucial. They do not know where to start, and their work environments rarely give them a clue.

Let us, therefore, find a place to begin. Build up your confidence by looking at what you've done so far. How can you develop your talent? Do you need a coach? Are you coachable?

If you work with someone like me, usually after two-to-four sessions, you get a path and decide some action to take—this was our friend Bear's discovery. He developed magnificently during the course of three months. For some people, the path is shorter and for others longer. No one follows someone else's path. When you find yours, however, the differences in attitude and outlook are remarkable.

The process works similarly for more established talent. Even people with a successful track record suffer from a lack of confidence when new challenges appear.

Established Talent

Today's great challenge for established leaders is the generation of emerging leaders. That's right, the old find themselves befuddled by the young. We think this is a new problem caused by coddling, entitlements, smart phones, Facebook, and other misplaced complaints, but that is nonsense. The new has always challenged the old.

Executives often find themselves stumped by this energetic, young, and very large demographic. Some retreat, some grow angry, others defensive, some adapt, and a few thrive. Why the difference? Confidence.

My clients consistently say: "We didn't do it this way when I was coming up. Twenty-five, thirty-five years ago, things were different." Of course, things were different! You were different! The world was different!

One client (an executive) worried about promoting the wrong person, losing a valued customer or a high-performing employee, understanding how technology may disrupt her industry, learning the latest software, increasing revenue, retaining market share, regulatory compliance, avoiding unnecessary taxation, and answering 200 emails while managing her nine direct reports. About the time she thought the dam would surely break, a young IT professional handed her a small box containing a device that claimed to make her life easier but really just gave her something new to learn (another task). After two days, she learned that the new device came with a task manager that was preloaded with twenty-five more things to do.

She made more money that she ever thought possible, but had no time to enjoy it.

She found herself daydreaming about retirement, and told me it sounded like death, but work was already killing her, so why not? As she looked toward retiring, she worried that the next person she promoted would fumble the work and tarnish her legacy. Her lack of confidence created tension that lowered her confidence further despite years of high achievement.

She was particularly upset when two young managers quit. She personally created their development plan, and the company spent about $40,000 on these two. She felt like she'd failed by not keeping them around. She wanted out of future hiring decisions, saying, "The risk to my reputation is not worth it, Jack."

Failure is not the right word. What we are talking about is feeling that people do not appreciate your sacrifice of time and money. They leave and you're still there trying to find new people to fill their position. You wonder how you made such a mistake in promoting the wrong person, and your confidence takes a hit.

My established clients most often complain that the younger generation lacks loyalty. At a deeper level, these experienced performers lack confidence in themselves to create something that lasts, and they blame the entire generation and American social structure for their problem. After batting this around with their friends, they no longer believe in the system they created. Executive often lack confidence in their ability to guide their organization given all the changes they observe, and when confidence fades, they disengage. Disengagement is new for them, and it further erodes their confidence.

In the case of my executive friend, her confidence returned in about three months, but not without a fight. She had to dig very deep to discover the thing within herself that was causing confidence to drop and disengagement to set it.

Defining confidence

Confidence is a belief that one can do what they set out to do. It's an energetic emotion that creates some stress. "Can I really play at this level?" The question requires confidence to pass from speculation to action, and on to successful completion.

If you take that emotion and let it percolate a bit so it gets into the reasoning part of the brain, it becomes more logical. Then, the person will realize, "Because of the things I've done in the past, I can do these things in the future." Meanwhile, there's tension and with tension comes misconception.

Misconceptions

One of the biggest misconceptions comes from not understanding how the brain works. One of the greatest discoveries of my life is that belief leads to confidence, confidence leads to action, and action over time leads to success. If a person does not believe they can do something, their brain starts proving the belief true as though a voice were repeating: "You aren't good enough," and it sabotages their goal.

People seem to think confidence is something they can buy from a book or a mentor. That is a myth. Confidence builds from action, and for most people, it builds very, very slowly. The way to build confidence is incrementally; with small steps beginning with whatever one can do today. Add new pieces by learning from books and wise advisors. If you want to speed it up, be open and teachable, and hire a coach! Sports, entertainment, and entrepreneurial heroes all hire coaches to speed up their learning.

Practice what you learn by taking action and by teaching others what you learned. Doing so sinks the new information deeper in your mind, and adds to your confidence.

What you learn will do nothing more than help you take the next step. It is literally the next step, which is often small, but still advances toward the goal. I'm sure you will agree that over time, enough small steps toward a goal will result in achieving the goal and building more confidence!

I remember working with an athlete who wanted to go from the type of races she was running to a much, much more difficult race. Her logic was, "I will train and train and train. I'll do more than I ever have." She had a terrible race.

She came to me and said, "I really lacked confidence." She believed she could do it in training, but she didn't believe she could do it in the race. That's why she finished near the back. As soon as she changed her belief, she raced again with no additional training and came in second place. The third time, fourth. The fifth time, third. The sixth time, she won.

Her confidence was the only thing that changed. The myth is that training and development takes the place of actually taking action toward a goal. Why do so many people attend seminars and read books but lack confidence? They fear action.

FEAR

Fear is an emotion designed to protect us. It keeps us from doing stupid things that endanger our lives.

Fear is an important part of the brain's design. An individual has a belief and beliefs charge up emotions, like fear. In the right place, fear rules to keeps us safe. Fear keeps me out of dark alleys. It wakes me up when I hear a noise in the middle of the night.

Sometimes, those fears of a creeping burglar turn out to be a noisy ice maker. My brain does not know the difference between a real and a perceived threat. It treats them both as something to fear.

If I'm trying to do something new, then my brain will try to protect me from bad feelings that come from failing. It will tell me: "Don't try for that promotion. What if you're passed over? Then, you're going to feel terrible."

Fear may save life, but to have a good life demands risk. Fear—really, it's false fear—prevents someone from risk. If I know that, I can say, "Wait a minute. There is nothing to be afraid of here. I might fail, but what if I succeed!"

If one spends time thinking of all the things they've achieved in the past to give them confidence, then eventually fear calms down. In other words, you can control it. It takes a little practice, but fear is controllable. When you get fear under control, what do you think happens to confidence? It soars.

I mentioned the role of coaching. Perhaps my story will help you understand my confidence.

COACHING

I started a coaching business because people kept telling me that I was really good at it. To some people that statement sounds arrogant. Do not confuse arrogance with confidence. It makes perfect sense to choose a profession at which one excels.

My confidence evolved as my skill increased. It started when I flunked out of college—a point when my confidence was in the gutter. Back then, the university assigned a time to report to the dean about one's scholastic dismissal.

I marched into the dean's office and whined about working a full-time job. I whined about the lousy professors. The dean just said, "Mr. Allen, the University of Texas does not care about your personal problems." That was the best advice I ever received.

I took it across campus to another dean's office. That dean asked if I wanted to learn. I did, and he spent a few minutes helping me understand how to manage my time.

On the way home, I ran into a football player I knew from class. I told him what happened, and he said something like: "Man, coach would never let that happen to us. We're constantly hearing about how to make grades." That's when I realized that those guys also had full-time jobs, but they made their grades—maybe I needed a coach.

I'd been listening to some self-help tapes and called the author. Lewis Timberlake became my coach for $100 per month, which was more than my rent and a lot more than I could afford. My Dad's reaction was so loud that I did not tell anyone else.

I told my boss I needed more hours. I would frame a house one day, pull weeds the next, and clean a house over the weekend. As my coach helped me understand goals and the other elements of personal development, my confidence grew. I returned to school, and made the dean's list.

Flunking out was not because I lacked intelligence; it was because I lacked confidence. I believed that because of family issues and laziness during my last year of high school, I had little confidence that I could succeed at the university level.

Once my confidence went up, my grades followed. That's the role of a good coach: to teach, inquire, observe, and to offer feedback and accountability. I paid $1,200 for coaching. I estimate that investment has paid me back about $2,000,000. That's a pretty good return on investment, isn't it?

The last decade or so, I've studied how the brain works. It's my geeky hobby: neuroscience and motivation; how we overcome fear and setbacks.

A few years ago, I was beginning a month-long teaching assignment in Africa. As it happened, some of my luggage was delayed and a book on the coaching profession was all I had to read. By the third chapter I realized I'd practiced coaching for years and seen great results. Next thing you know, an opportunity appeared to take my practice to an even higher level by starting Dynamic Coaching, and now the opportunities come from every direction. Fear was there—it never left—but I know how to control it. That gives me more confidence.

CONCLUSION

My research shows the progression. Start with gratitude for what you have to defeat fear of not having enough. Figure out what's causing your confidence to wane, and if that thing is a real or imagined fear. Remove fake fears, and replace them with belief in what's true about you based on what you've achieved. Take action toward what you want (even tiny steps in the right direction will get you to a better place). Keep taking action until you get it.

Hire a coach to speed things up or to help you get unstuck. Reading is a slower path to develop confidence, but it still works.

There is a way to decrease your confidence: do nothing. But that doesn't sound like you, does it?

HOW TO FIND OUT MORE

Sign up for your free consultation at www.jackallenphd.com/appointments

◇◇◇

Jack Allen, Ph.D., owns Dynamic Coaching, LLC in Austin. He is an expert in organizational culture development, ethics, motivation, and neuroscience. Over the last 25 years, he has spoken to over 100,000 people with audiences in every major US city as well as Ireland, Kenya, Rwanda, and Guatemala. Jack has inspired groups from 25 to 2500 in venues from a sweaty tent in Africa to the air-conditioned Georgia Dome in Atlanta; from a cozy living room in Dublin, Ireland to a Grand Ballroom in Washington, DC. His humorous, candid approach opens audiences to new thoughts on old problems. You'll find laughter, inspiration, actions to move in a better direction, and you will be glad you called him.

From Ideas to Action

Patricia Selmo

"Genius is the ability to put into effect what is in your mind."
                                                        – F. Scott Fitzgerald

---

You have a great idea that you want to implement. Maybe it's a new business or a personal change or shift. Maybe it's a business teaching scuba diving, or you want to lose 50 pounds, or you have a message to get out into the world. The principles that work for any endeavor are the same. These foundational principles have been applied many times by many successful people. Sometimes, you might need to focus more on one than another, and the one more focused on might differ depending on the situation.

What follows is a framework that, if followed, will lead to your success.

KEY 1 — BLOOM WHERE YOU'RE PLANTED

Before launching into your idea or desire, take a breath and notice where you are. "The grass is not always greener...it still needs to be mowed!"

When a rocket-ship is launched or a gymnast jumps onto the balance beam, the thing that most helps them get to where they're going is the foundation they are launching or jumping from...the launchpad or platform. This platform provides them with a firm foundation, without which, they would not be able to get to their intended goal. It's simple physics: every action has an equal and opposite reaction. It provides the impetus to get things moving.

The same principle applies in life and business. For this reason, when trying to launch something new, the first thing we need to consider is our foundation. Is it strong enough to support this launch?

In 2012, I found myself living in Houston with my mom, back in the house I grew up in. My business was failing. I wanted to be anywhere except Houston, and basically felt like I should be much further along at the age of 47. I knew something needed to change, but I had no idea where to start, or what to do. I decided to take the advice of one of my favorite authors, SARK – who stated "Bloom where you're planted." Therefore, much as I hated to do that, (since that was NOT where I wanted to be planted), I did it. What that looked like was appreciation for where I was. I began to be truly grateful (see Key 6) for anything and everything I could think of in my present state.

This act shifted me enough to be able to build a strong enough foundation to lift off from, to make the change I wanted to make. The next part of this Key was to "Know Myself" better. Having gotten into the energy of blooming where I was, I could see all the resources I had at my disposal much better. I looked first at the "external" resources such as money, assets, other people.

Then, I made a list of the "internal" resources such as my values, skills and experience.

Arguably, the most important thing in life is to know yourself. The Ancient Greek aphorism "Know Thyself", was inscribed in the forecourt of the famous Temple of Apollo at Delphi, where it was believed that humans connected with the gods.

I believe this idea can open your awareness. When your awareness awakens to your true nature, it also opens myriad possibilities in the world.

Take a moment now to take stock of your life and truly know your platform.

KEY 2 — TAKE AIM: GET CLEAR AND DECIDE

One day in late February of 2012, I was laying in bed in my mom's house, and suddenly I opened my eyes and sat straight up in bed. I had a thought pop in my head with the intensity and clarity of an arrow finding its mark. The thought was "I have to be in Austin."

At that time, my daughter and son-in-law had been living there for several years. Now, this was not a conscious thought in the sense that I thought about it and logically came to that conclusion. This was a "Eureka!" moment that came out of nowhere and landed in my heart, where I knew it to be true. I made the decision right then that it would happen.

Key 2 is to make sure that this is the direction you want to head in. Even a rocket ship needs to be aimed.

If you are doing this for external reasons (someone else wants you to do it or you think it's a good idea because someone else told you it was), you might find that your heart doesn't sing when you think about it. If that is the case – dump it, right now!

As we go through life, we come in contact with many different situations, experiences, people and options. Not all of these are for our highest good. How do we know which path to follow, which decision to make? We can determine this by knowing our true nature – by remembering to keep that heart-centered connection open so we can hear, loud and clear, those messages that are meant for us.

Go within to do this to be sure it is a heart-centered idea. Sit with it for a while and notice the FEELINGS you feel when you think about it. How does it make you feel? If it makes you happy or excited, go for it!

KEY 3 — TAKE GUIDED ACTION

Now that you have a strong launchpad and are aimed in a clear direction, you are going to connect with the fuel to get you going; and you will tap into your internal GPS to keep you going in that direction.

Your GPS is called by many names. For the sake of simplicity I am going to be referring to it as intuition. What is intuition? It is the communication link you have, to something bigger than you that "knows" or can see the bigger picture. That "something bigger" that you are connecting with can be referred to by whatever name appeals to you and your belief system. This could be something spiritual such as God or the Divine, the Universe, Life or even just a part of yourself that "knows."

Know that you have access to this vast source of knowledge. You simply need to learn how to tune in to it and hear and understand the messages that you receive. These messages don't come as a blaring voice clearly delineating what it is you need to know or do. This voice has often been called the still, small voice, because it tends to come as a whisper. If you are really tuned in and open to receive these messages, you quickly realize that they are coming to you all the time through various means.

It wasn't until 3 days after that "Eureka" moment in my childhood bedroom, that my daughter called me with the news that I was going to become a grandmother in October! I know that I got that message before then, because I was connected and listening to something larger than me that knew even before she told me. Her call simply validated what I already "knew" on some level.

The next thing I did was to research what I needed to do get there. I took my skills and experience list from Key 1 and figured out what sort of job to look for. I interviewed people who did it. I talked to recruiters to help me find that position. I began to scope out places to live and talked to an apartment locator to help me find the perfect place. I did the practical, left-brain activities required to make the change.

Notice that I tapped into the internal GPS first, and that helped guide me to the next steps to take "externally/" Some of these things might be:

- Research your idea – has anyone else done it? What can you learn from them?

- What needs to happen to get this idea done? What order do these things go in?

- What are the tools/resources you need to accomplish it?

You'll find that when you practice living in this connected way, you may even get "inspiration" to follow a certain lead, or "coincidentally" bump into someone who can help with your idea.

When we take action, the universe reaches out to us in levels of magnitude to help us achieve what we are meant to do. It doesn't always come in the form we expect, so we need to pay attention. We need to ask, but we also need to act – not rashly, but in alignment with spiritual guidance. That means talk to spirit, soul, or higher self, but don't forget to listen as well!

KEY 4 — ACT AS IF

You've probably heard the idea of "like attracts like." In this Key, your aim is to make sure that the energy you are putting out into the world resonates with the vibration of your desires or idea. Really get into the feeling that your idea has already come to fruition. How do you act and what actions do you take if this is true?

In my effort to move to Austin, I began to "act as if" I lived in Austin. I did this by beginning to find all my service providers in Austin. For example, I found a new hairdresser, massage therapist and place of worship there, as though I already lived there. I even began to tell people (when it made sense) that I lived there. If there was something I normally did in Houston, if possible, I found a way to do it in Austin instead.

Create the space. Your environment is a reflection of your internal state. Make your space ready to receive your desires. This can include clearing clutter, making space in your closet to attract a new relationship, or space in your garage for that new car. It also refers to the space in your "head" – get into the mindset of someone who has accomplished this goal or idea. What does that person do differently than someone who hasn't?

Learn to say "No" or "Not right now." If you are not accustomed to saying the word, "NO," it can take time and practice to verbalize it. As with anything, the more we use discernment and practice, the easier it becomes. Using the clarity gained from the previous Keys; it becomes much easier to know when to say "no" and when to say "yes" to opportunities that present themselves to us.

Draw from the energy created in Key 2. That heart-centered fuel is what will get you through. I guarantee that when the going gets tough (and it will), you will need the heart and passion to be there to pull you through. Courage comes from the Latin word "cor" meaning heart. Your heart will provide the fuel you need to reach your goal.

In the six weeks it took me to get from idea to action (and success) in moving to Austin, what pulled me forward was the knowledge of the little being that was about to enter our world. I knew in my heart that I needed to be there for my daughter and grandchild. It gave me the faith necessary to put a deposit down on an apartment before finding the job that would sustain me.

Key 5 — Overcome Resistance

We've all experienced the "self-sabotage" that sometimes occurs when we outwardly say we want something - whether it's to lose weight or change careers. But, then sometimes, our actions don't match that declaration. Why do we resist something we say we want?

The reason can be explained by acknowledging at the most basic level that we all have both a conscious and a subconscious mind. Our conscious mind contains the thoughts we are aware—or conscious—of. The subconscious mind is like the autopilot of our belief systems gained through authority figures, parents, teachers and events we've "learned from" in the past.

Resistance is basically our sub-conscious mind trying to protect us. The job of the subconscious mind is to look for danger and keep us from doing things that it perceives might harm us.

What does resistance look like? Pretty much doing anything and everything except what we say we want to do or accomplish. Sometimes the subconscious can come up with some great arguments about why we're doing all these other things as well. These "stories" we tell ourselves can keep us stuck for a very long time - some people stay stuck in these narratives their whole lives. If you're reading this, you probably don't want to be one of them.

Very often when we hit resistance, there is an underlying belief or fear that is stopping us from moving forward. When this happens, ask yourself "What fear or belief is driving this?" "What am I afraid might happen if I continue forward in this way?" Continue asking "Why?" or "And then what?" until you get to the core fear or belief driving your resistance.

Hypnosis can be a great way to get you into a relaxed state where you can easily access your inner conscious. From there it becomes much easier to find the original event that created the fear and erase it. Please know that I am not referring to stage hypnosis where people cluck like chickens! I am referring to consulting hypnosis by trained professionals that adhere to ethical standards, with the intention of helping people overcome limiting beliefs and habits. Please go to a professional organization such as the National Guild of Hypnotists (http://ngh.net/) to find a reputable practitioner.

Another method is to write down any beliefs or fears you are experiencing and reframe them to something more positive. You can even use a visual of moving that belief or thought to the back of your mind where it is less accessible. Then visualize placing the more supporting thought in the front of your mind where you can access it more easily.

KEY 6 — PRACTICE GRATITUDE

Remember that whatever your idea or goal, it's the journey not the destination. Key 6 is all about gratitude for where we are and what it took to get us here. We've come full circle from Key 1 to realize that it all begins and ends with Gratitude. I've heard that the difference between a highly aware and evolved person and enlightenment is the act of gratitude for anything and everything always.

Be in the present – this is all any of us really has. Keep your eye on the goal, but stay in the present and enjoy it! Give gratitude for it and take pleasure in it. Believe me, this simple practice will keep going towards that goal when you encounter obstacles along the way. I sometimes think the universe tests us when we make a declaration about what we want – it sends us obstacles to see if we really mean what we say. Each of those moments is a great opportunity to check in with yourself and see if you still want what you say you want. You might decide you don't, or that it needs to be redirected a bit, or that you are still going gang-busters towards it. Any of these responses are fine. Just be AWARE — and you can't do that if you're not in the moment.

Sometimes when we are in the middle of a transition, or new idea, we are so intent on what COULD be that we fail to notice what is. The very first thing to do is to notice where you are now, and be GRATEFUL for all of it — even the things you are wanting to change.

85

Remember, the first thing I did was to take note of where I was. I had a roof over my head, and it was pretty much rent-free. I knew where my next meal was coming from (maybe a little too much if you get my drift), both my parents were still alive, I had a wonderful circle of friends and a supportive networking group. Things could definitely be worse. This small act, changed my energy and outlook just enough that I could begin to think differently.

As Albert Einstein said, "We cannot solve our problems with the same level of thinking that created them."

Begin today to create a list of 100 things you are grateful for - right now, in one sitting. Then, set this up as a regular habit or ritual that you do daily by listing 3–5 things you are grateful for every evening before going to bed or in the morning upon rising.

What I learned in my journey from Houston to Austin — and correspondingly from idea to action is that these keys work. Are the keys simple? Yes! Are they easy? Not always. But this is where getting into the vibration... the Flow, will help carry you along.

What was different for me when I moved from Houston to Austin, compared to all the countless times I set goals, made vision boards, started weight loss programs? The difference was the embodiment of these principles.

I know you have it in you to do this. You would not be given the idea without the means to accomplish it. You are powerful beyond belief and you can create anything your heart desires. As Maya Angelou reminds us: "The most important thing, beyond discipline and creativity is daring to dare."

You can do this and I am here to believe in you even when you don't.

<><><><><><><><><><><><><><><><><><><><><><><><><><><><><><><><><><><><><><><><><><><><>

Patricia Selmo is a former aerospace engineer who now helps individuals and companies gain clarity, navigate transitions and turn their many ideas into actionable plans. She uses her 25+ years of corporate change and project management experience combined with her strengths in listening and pattern-finding, and her written, verbal and graphic communications skills to help individuals and teams make the difference they are meant to make in the world. She is a content and product creation guide, certified consulting hypnotist and cofounder of Intentional Edge (www.IntentionalEdge.com) helping teens and parents navigate to success. As a Certified Visual Coach™, she loves to inspire others to tap into their own creative juices for inspiration and success. She can be found helping teams visually capture their strategic visions and ideas at www.PatriciaSelmo.com; and helping coaches, consultants, authors and speakers put their ideas into keynotes, books, programs and workshops at www.BrainstormingBreakthroughs.com.

A Question of Culture

Sharon Schweitzer

When we marry, most of us discover that our spouse's family has a different set of expectations, values, and beliefs, ranging from broad topics, such as boundaries to specific subjects such as shared holidays. Invariably, these are different from the way we were raised. If we can reconcile our own values with those of our new extended family, we avoid the potential culture clash; if not, and things escalate, the end result can be unpleasant. The same holds true in business.

J.B. (not his real name) is a factory owner in Chennai, in southern India, whose mid-sized business produces revenues of around $250 million a year and has two joint venture agreements. One relationship, with a German company, has happily lasted 18 years. The other, with a U.S. company, he wants to draw to a close, because of their less than desirable approach to doing business.

For example, on one occasion, J.B. wanted to spend $5,000 to manufacture a tool for a particular project and was questioned at length by his U.S. partners as to why he didn't just buy the tool from vendors overseas. J.B. responded that these vendors did not allow him to purchase a single item, only items in bulk, which he felt was wasteful and would incur unnecessary shipping costs. Overall, it was going to be considerably less expensive to make the part. After further laborious discussions, his U.S. partners reluctantly agreed.

ACCESS TO ASIA

In contrast, J.B.'s experience with the Germans is such that, "If I make a request, they will ask me if that is the best solution in my opinion. If I say yes, they trust my expertise." Why would J.B.'s experience with the Germans be so different from the experience with his U.S.

partners? In short: cultural differences. But before examining this example further, let's explore what we mean by the word culture.

We use the word culture in many different contexts, including countries, organizations, and groups, and we talk about cultural misunderstandings, cultural clashes, cultural fit, and even culture shock. However, books and articles focused on cultural topics often neglect to define the term. Perhaps that is not surprising, considering the complexities involved in explaining culture.

Culture was originally an agricultural term, used in the Middle Ages, stemming from the Latin word cultura, meaning the care, cultivation, or honoring of the land; we still talk about cultivating plants. But since the early nineteenth century, culture also became associated with the beliefs, values, and customs of different civilizations. Culture is complex and hard to pin down with a single definition because it encompasses many sub-components.

Culture

"Culture is the accumulation of life experiences spanning generations."
Sheida Hodge, Global Smarts

One place to start is to compare culture with similar but not synonymous concepts, such as identity, nationhood, values, and norms. Renowned intercultural researcher and the author of numerous books on this topic, including Culture's Consequences, Geert Hofstede advises that culture is distinct from identity: Your identity has more to do with where and with whom you belong, as in national identity, or your identity within a particular group. Culture, on the other hand, is concerned with "the collective programming of the mind that distinguishes the members of one group or category of people from another." In that regard, Hofstede considers culture to consist of "the unwritten rules of the social game." These are the rules we learn from observing what goes on in our specific environment, together with the learning we get from others, rather than something we are born knowing, such as the human propensity for smiling, or the fear of death, which are innate across all races.

A Question of Culture

Some of the earliest influences of Hofstede and others stemmed from research conducted by cultural anthropologists. For example, Florence Kluckhohn and Fred Strodtbeck's (1961) value orientations theory postulated six different types of beliefs, influences, and relationships. Kluckhohn and Strodtbeck differentiated them according to the following dimensions:

- Relationship with nature— especially the need for control

- Social structure— whether focused mostly on individuals or groups

- Appropriate goals— being or doing

- Time— past (traditions), present (current circumstances), or future (desires/goals)

- Basis of human nature— good or evil

- Conception of space — public or private

These anthropologically sound dimensions speak to all forms of community, including our business lives.

Culture is not synonymous with nationhood for the simple reason that just under 200 countries exist in the world today, whereas, according to Richard Lewis, there are some 700 national and regional cultures. Additionally, culture is not synonymous with concepts such as norms and values; it encompasses them.

PATTERN INTERRUPT

> *"Many Japanese executives are reserved, polite, quiet, and rarely display emotion. Somewhere there is probably a loud, boisterous, gesticulating Japanese manager who is as emotional and imperious as any prima donna. Just because we haven't met him (or her) doesn't mean that no such person exists."*
> — **Terri Morrison and Wayne A. Conaway**

Many commentators, including Fons Trompenaars, Geert Hofstede, George Simons, and Sheida Hodge have represented culture as a multi-layered model. Depictions of these representations are either in the form of concentric circles or an iceberg, and highlight the difference between the cultural components of which we are aware and those that are subconscious. Think of a peach with three layers: the outer skin, the flesh, and the innermost pit or stone.

This approach aligns with Edward T. Hall's three levels of culture, outlined in The Dance of Life: The Other Dimension of Time. The outer skin represents the conscious or visible manifestations of culture, including literature, food, music, fashion, and art. These are often visible, such as the kimono in Japan, the sari in India or the hijab in Malaysia. The middle layer or flesh comprises norms and values that are often unknown to people outside that culture. Examples include authority, consensus, family, modesty, personal space, and spirituality.

The innermost pit or stone represents the hidden or subconscious assumptions held by a culture about how the world works, such as fatalism, environmental control, and notions of time. Consider the analogy of a goldfish in water. That medium is pivotal to the way the goldfish lives and breathes until the water evaporates or the bowl breaks. This is similar to the culture shock that many experience when moving to a different culture.

Let's now consider the less-than-desirable relationship J.B. has with his U.S. partners and contrast that with his more satisfactory dealings with the German company. How can this be, when you would expect there to be greater similarities between Germany and the U.S. than between Germany and India?

Many factors are involved in business dealings with culturally different partners. One model was developed by Geert Hofstede, who, having analyzed cultural differences since the late 1960s, identified six "dimensions of national cultures," three of which are especially pertinent to the J.B. Example.

The first of these is what Hofstede identified as uncertainty avoidance, meaning the degree to which a culture is tolerant of ambiguity and feels comfortable with unknown situations. Ironically, the United States and India are closer to each other in terms of their comfort with uncertainty than either of them is with the Germans. However, as Hofstede explains, the Germans compensate for their desire to avoid uncertainty by relying on others' expertise. This aligns well with the Indian preference for power, another of Hofstede's dimensions. In India, power is unequally distributed throughout the culture, with the boss (J.B.) being the final decision maker. When the Germans asked J.B. if his suggestion was the best option, and he confirmed that it was, they accepted his opinion. The Germans were presumably able to reduce their level of uncertainty by giving credence to the power differential that J.B. is afforded in Indian society as the head of the company.

The third relevant dimension to mention here is that of short-term or long-term orientation. Germany and the U.S. are both examples of the Western tendency for seeking results in the short-term. In comparison, many Asian cultures, such as India, prefer to take a long-term view. As one Indian executive explained:

"By taking the long view, Indians are apt to make allowances for the fact that not everything is always going to go to plan. That includes the fact that early on in a relationship there are bound to be hiccups. This is only to be expected, given the complexity of human interactions. Yet it's remarkable to us how Americans hold to the belief in one Truth, whereas we Indians know there to be many Truths, each one applicable according to the context in which it is applied."

Again, why is there more alignment between the Indian and German executives, and more friction between J.B. and his U.S. partners? Perhaps because of J.B.'s industry experience and expertise, the Germans received assurance that their short-term needs would be met. Trust is highly relevant here. Former President Ronald Reagan's comment, "Trust but verify," is anathema to Indians, who would not consider the need for verification to be indicative of trust.

WHY THIS? WHY NOW?

Cultural considerations vary geographically in many countries. In the U.S., for example, conducting business in the Midwest is different from doing so in Texas or California. As the former CEO of Coca-Cola, Doug Ivester, said, "As economic borders come down, cultural barriers go up, presenting new challenges and opportunities in business." According to Athanasios Vamvakidis, an economist in the International Monetary Fund's Asia and Pacific Department, "Alongside the globalization process, countries have been increasing their regional economic links through regional trade agreements."

As economic borders have come down, what about the cultural barriers? The authors of Getting China and India Right, Anil K. Gupta and Haiyan Wang, stated that any organization looking to make progress in these markets needs to embrace the kind of long-term orientation typical of India and China and rarely found in Western countries:

According to Gupta and Wang: "Most companies will find that their existing knowledge about how to succeed in other markets teaches them little about how to succeed in China and India. If they want to aim for market leadership rather than merely skimming the cream at the top, they will need to engage in considerable learning from scratch."

With that in mind, as you discover a little more about the ways U.S. culture compares with Asian cultures, what you find out will create a baseline for understanding the different perspectives among these cultures and help create deeper, more lasting, and more trusted relationships. After all, in order to know how to relate to other cultures, you first need to know where you are standing.

So, here's a question for you:

Who Are "Americans"?

The term American is very broad and includes the inhabitants of Central, Latin, North, and South America. It doesn't just refer to people who live in the U.S., as the following table shows.

North America: A continent with 23 countries (Antigua and Barbuda; Bahamas; Barbados; Belize; Canada; Costa Rica; Cuba; Dominica; Dominican Republic; El Salvador; Grenada; Guatemala; Haiti; Honduras; Jamaica; Mexico; Nicaragua; Panama; St. Kitts & Nevis; St. Lucia; St. Vincent and the Grenadines; Trinidad and Tobago; United States) and dozens of possessions and territories

South America: A continent with 12 countries (Argentina; Bolivia; Brazil; Chile; Columbia; Ecuador; Guyana; Peru; Paraguay; Suriname; Uruguay; Venezuela) and three territories (Falkland Islands; French Guiana; Galapagos Islands)

Central America: A region comprising seven countries (Belize; Costa Rica; El Salvador; Guatemala; Honduras; Nicaragua; Panama).

Latin America: A region comprising: Mexico, Central America, South America, and "the islands of the Caribbean whose inhabitants speak a Romance language."

There are numerous Americans in the world who have cultural customs and ways of interacting that are quite different from those found in the U.S. This is why, for this chapter, we have elected to use a more specific term and refer throughout to U.S. Americans.

Sharon Schweitzer, J.D., is an award winning entrepreneur, a cultural communication expert, corporate trainer, modern manners expert and the founder of Access to Culture. With deep international experience, travel to more than 70 countries, and her accreditation in intercultural management from the HOFSTEDE Centre, she also serves as a Chinese Ceremonial Dining Etiquette Specialist in the documentary series Confucius was a Foodie, on Nat Geo People. Her Amazon #1 Best Selling book in International Business, Access to Asia: Your Multicultural Business Guide, now in its third printing, was named to Kirkus Reviews' Best Books of 2015. She's a winner of the British Airways International Trade Award at the 2016 Greater Austin Business Awards. She works with global organizations, law firms, universities and executive teams, athletes and highly motivated individuals providing practical techniques to improve business communication and increase revenue.

The Five Be's for Entrepreneurs

Mickey Addison

Learn from others' mistakes, you don't have time to make them all yourself - GK Chesterton

Who do you want to be? That's the fundamental question every person, and particularly entrepreneurs, should be asking themselves every day. Answering that question gives us a destination to journey toward. Of course, reaching our goals and becoming a healthy, successful person requires daily re-commitment. That daily commitment is a *positive* action we can take to keep ourselves aligned and moving toward our goals. The Five Be's is a straightforward guide to making and keeping that commitment to your goals and to yourself.

The Five Be's is more than just a rule set or formula, it's a positive vision of the kind of person who is successful and healthy. Imagine living in a world where all you ever hear is "no" and "don't"? It seems silly to phrase our coaching and guidance in those words, but let's face it: that's what most people do, even to themselves. That approach is like having the bumpers installed on a bowling lane. Those bumpers cover the gutters so young bowlers can get the ball to the end of the lane and take down some pins. Usually the ball ends up careening down the alley bouncing between the bumpers and if the bowler is lucky, striking a few pins at the end. Without defining our destination, the kind of people we want to be, we're simply bouncing back and forth between the bumpers in life.

There's a better way.

From the time we're very young we're presented with a list of "don'ts" to set boundaries.

To be sure young people get the lion's' share of the boundary setting, but every society and organization has its list of what you can't do. Boundaries are necessary, but a leader's job is to inspire people to group and individual achievement so the job can't end at "don't." We have to be able to articulate a positive view of where we want our teammates and followers to be. If we don't then we're not leading anyone anywhere in particular we're just screaming out "row!" without telling them *where* they're rowing.

I vividly recall sitting with my fellow Air Force commanders as we discussed the various discipline issues we were dealing with and think, "when have we told these people who we want them to *be*?" That's the difference between *inspiration* and *discouragement*. Good leaders, and successful entrepreneurs, *inspire* people—stakeholders, investors, teammates, and even themselves. In my time as a commander and leader in the Air Force, I found it necessary and even profitable to articulate this vision of who I wanted my Airmen to *be* as a companion to the boundaries we established to guide their behavior. That's where the "Five Be's" comes in: its who I want to be, and who I want the people around me to be. It's a positive vision for a person to "Aim High" so they can reach their goals and be "all they can be" in their work and their life.

The "Five Be's" are: Be Proud of Who You Are, Be Free, Be Virtuous, Be Balanced, and Be Courageous.

BE PROUD OF WHO YOU ARE

As a commander I used to remind my Airmen they were part of the mightiest military force on the planet: the US Air Force. They could be justly proud of their contribution to keeping America safe, and for what they contribute to the joint team. Similarly, leaders should instill pride in their teams for the work they're doing, whether that's in business or the public sector. Leaders must remind employees they're work is important: because it's noble and selfless, because it's providing an important service, or because it's putting food on the table-whatever the reason-the boss must give people a reason to come to work beyond "I said so." A sense of mission goes a long way to making the team cohesive and productive.

But organizational pride only goes so far, and leaders must help individuals cultivate their own sense of self-worth. Everyone has something in their past or upbringing to be proud of; help them see it. It could be their sense of belonging to their family, or accomplishments in sports or business, or as an expert in their field; whatever the reason, remind them to be proud of who they are. The more people see themselves as valuable, and the more they are treated as valuable, the stronger the team. A chain is only as strong as the weakest link, so a chain made of very strong links is a tough one!

For the individual and the entrepreneur, it's vital to remember that everyone has something to contribute. Remember to look for teammates and contributions in unlikely places. Going to the same well over and over again may seem comfortable, but doing so will guarantee the same answers. History is replete with businesses that failed to adapt and subsequently failed. Don't be one of them because you diminished yourself or others when you didn't recognize their value.

BE FREE

There is an idea popular in 21st century society that "freedom" means "doing whatever I please." That's not freedom: it's "license." *Authentic freedom* is being able to choose those things that make you and those around you better, that improve your community as well as yourself. It *doesn't* mean there are no limits, it *does* mean leaders place limits on our teams and ourselves to keep them/us healthy and productive.

The metaphor I use often to describe this idea is how gravity works. Because of the "Law of Gravity" I am free to move about the Earth confident I understand the "rules" and without flying off into space. I might "escape" Earth's gravity to get into orbit, but that smooth arc I travel through space is because of gravity. I can even use gravity to "slingshot" my spacecraft to faster speeds around the solar system! However, without gravity I would be unable to move or travel: I'd simply be flung off the Earth and into space moving in a straight line until I ran into something else. I'm free because I'm "bound" by gravity!

So it is in the personal realm. If I am surrendering my energy to something that prevents me from achieving my goals, or something that makes me unhealthy physically or emotionally, then I'm not free~even if I am freely choosing the thing that is bad for me. Leaders have to create an environment where choosing the good is encouraged and even celebrated. Being free personally, and maintaining an environment where others can also be free, is a prerequisite to having a healthy and productive team.

In addition to the usual vices that drag us down, entrepreneurs can become enslaved to their work. When you're invested in an idea and a business, it's *very* easy to allow it to consume you entirely leaving nothing for yourself or your family. Success in life is a journey, so using up all your energy or allowing something unhealthy to consume you will prevent you from achieving the very thing you've committed yourself to achieving. I used to tell my fellow Airmen they'd only be in the Air Force for part of their lives, but their family is for their whole lives. That's true for the entrepreneur as well. Sacrificing long term happiness for short term gain is a poor life decision.

Be Virtuous

Modern society has distanced itself from the Classical Ideal of virtue, but the ancient Classical Cardinal Virtues are as important today as they ever were. I maintain keeping to the virtues of: *Prudence* (using good judgment), *Justice* (being fair), *Temperance* (not overdoing it), and *Fortitude* (strength to endure trials gracefully) is particularly important for leaders to both model and cultivate.

When each person knows and understands *as a given* the honesty and virtue of their coworkers, minds and hearts are free to think bigger thoughts. Put another way, when each person expects the leader and their teammates to treat each other honorably they can commit more fully to the team's mission. Moreover, and more to the point, striving to live a virtuous life is both good for us as leaders and good for us as people. When people strive for what's good for them, they are then healthy in mind and spirit and able to contribute more fruitfully to whatever their organization has for them to do.

Most people know and understand what's right and wrong, notwithstanding the occasional human train wreck or psychopath. Moral philosophers and theologians call that innate knowledge of right and wrong, the Natural Law. Giving labels to that knowledge is important—hence the need for the Cardinal Virtues. They honestly aren't that hard to understand. *Prudence* is merely doing the right thing at the appropriate time; *Justice* is giving others' their due and being honest; *Temperance* is moderating your own selfish desires to achieve your goals; and *Fortitude* is having the courage and inner strength to keep going even when life is tough.

Long term success depends on virtue. Anyone can be successful in the short term by lying, cheating, or stealing, but those people usually run out of luck and friends in the long term. Prisons and divorce courts are full of those people. People who are successful, happy, and healthy into old age are almost always the virtuous ones.

Be Balanced

In my experience, the most effective leaders were the most balanced. They made time for work, family, mind, body, and spirit. The results I observed were people with seemingly endless stores of energy and high achievement. They were disciplined and focused, and kept their priorities in what I believe are the right order. In a world where sometimes the sole measure of merit is the number of hours worked and the bottom line, it's refreshing to know leaders who prioritize all sides of their personality rather than sacrificing their families or health on the altar of success.

In the military we have a saying, "everyone gets a pink slip eventually" which means although many serve for decades, at some point we have to hang the uniform up and return to civilian life. Our personal lives and families *don't* get a "pink slip"–we're in those our entire lives–so maintaining a healthy balance is crucial to arriving at retirement as an intact person. I think that same metaphor can be extended to all walks of life: no matter what your profession or business, at the end you have your personal health and the affection of those around you. A truly successful leader finds a way to achieve the results they seek while still striving to be "all they can be."

Like all other professions, balance is critical for long term success of entrepreneurs. Make time to work out and eat real food. Work requires energy and a sound body; any athlete will tell you they can tell a difference in their performance when they're not sleeping, training, or eating properly. Spend time improving your mind: read books, think and talk about big things, be constantly learning. Lastly, feed your human spirit with good things: beauty, art, worship, and spend time in silence from time to time. Maintaining a good balance of mind, body, and spirit.

BE COURAGEOUS

Entrepreneurship requires courage, sometimes both *physical* and *moral* courage. While most won't be required to face bullets or burning buildings, entrepreneurs risk their fortunes and sometimes their families' financial security to make their dreams come true. Many entrepreneurs fail, some fail spectacularly, so drawing courage from the well within ourselves is central to being successful. Once the initial energy and excitement drains away and the new venture enters the "Trough of Sorrows," it takes *courage* to stay on course and do the hard work required for success.

Of the two types of courage, physical and moral courage, moral courage is usually in the shortest supply. Risk taking comes with the leadership territory. Decisions leaders make can have far reaching effects on the organization and the people in it, so there's often immense pressure on leaders to get it right. Unfortunately, the pressure to get to the right answer leads some to make *no* decisions. In organizations with "paralysis by analysis," leaders who have the moral courage to take risks and make decisions can take a struggling organization and make them a high achieving one.

Courage to make decisions is only part of the equation, however. As leaders, we have to make the *right* decisions, especially in situations where ethics are involved. Do we do the inspection or merely sign off on the form? Are we truthful with clients and teammates about our limitations or do we say anything to get the sale? In the end, half-truths and half-done tasks harm us more than they harm others. Leaders have to set the example and do what's right; not merely because "everyone is looking," but to be sure we don't mortgage our own soul to get a sale. Having moral courage is good for everyone, but it's also good for each of us.

WRAP-UP

So those are the "Five Be's"—Be Proud, Free, Virtuous, Balanced, Courageous. It's a positive vision of the sort of person I want to model, and the sort of people I want around me. The Five Be's are a straightforward guide to a healthy and successful life. The question we began with still remains: Who do you want to be?

Colonel Mickey Addison, USAF (ret), believes everyone can reach high performance if inspired and led. He's the author of The Five Be's, Leading Leaders, and Mickey's Rules for Leaders. As an Air Force officer, Mickey managed national portfolios totaling billions of dollars. He's presented on dozens of topics to senior leaders in government, industry, state and federal government, and worked with international business and government executives and in a dozen countries in Asia, Europe, and the Middle East.

The Gorilla Says Yes!
Innovation from a Singing Telegram Performer

Mardi Wareham

What would you do if you saw a gorilla walking down the hall at work? Not a real gorilla, a person in a big black hairy gorilla costume.

What if the person inside the costume was your company's Communications and Marketing Director? This is a true story of innovation: how I went from being a Marketing Director to CEO and chief performer at my own singing telegram company. The secret to my transformation? I just kept saying, "YES!"

I also kept saying, "I hope I don't get fired," because I had launched my company while I already had a job as Marketing Director at a Methodist church in Austin. I started off with just one costume — black formal attire — and quickly added a gorilla, a bright yellow chicken, a ukulele-playing Hawaiian princess, Queen Elizabeth and The Blonde Bombshell.

When the customers booked me, they chose the character and song they wanted, and the location where the telegram would take place. Generally, they hired me to celebrate a friend or relative's birthday, anniversary or other special occasion.

A LITTLE MONKEY BUSINESS

Here was the scenario: I would be working away on the church's weekly newsletter and when the lunch hour arrived, I would throw on my gorilla suit or chicken costume, drive like a crazy person to the telegram location, belt out "It Had to Be You" and get everyone to sing "Happy Birthday," then head back to the church to finish the newsletter. I remember giggling as I passed the elderly church members in the hallway wearing my costumes.

Normally I'm a strict rule follower – I grew up in Canada, a whole nation of rule followers – but here I was following my own dream, breaking the rules and ignoring the scowling face of the Director of Worship who thought it undignified for me to cruise the church halls in my telegram costumes. (He may have had a point.)

You too can follow your dream and say **YES!**

JULIA CHILD COMES CALLING

I'll give you another example of how I said yes.

One day an older gentleman called my business phone and asked, "It's not on your website but would you do Julia Child, the chef? My daughter loves cooking and she's always watching reruns of Julia's TV show. Could you put something together?"

I already had a Mom-type character so I had the pearls that Julia was famous for wearing while cooking. I already had a Queen Elizabeth character, and her accent was similar to Julia's so I knew I could do a decent impersonation.

Julia herself had died in 2004 but I had recently watched the movie, "Julie and Julia," starring Meryl Streep as Julia Child. It was a hoot!

"Yes!" I said. "I will do Julia!"

THE CREATION OF A NEW CHARACTER

I used what I already had in order to create something new. There were no venture capitalists knocking on my door. No millionaires on reality TV shows looking at funding me.

Here's what I did:

I watched videos of Julia's shows from the 1960s and Dan Akroyd's famous skit on the TV show *Saturday Night Live* in which he mimics Julia. I read biographical books about Julia's life. It seemed like anyone who had ever known Julia wrote a book about her. She made an impression! Well, she was 6'2"!

I haunted thrift stores to buy a costume. I ordered chef's hats from a restaurant supply store. I bought a realistic-looking large red plastic lobster and a crab.

I wrote out a skit — a mock cooking lesson – and practiced it at home and on friends.

I found and memorized a spoof of the song *My Favorite Things* that Julie Andrews sang in *The Sound of Music* movie. A friend of Julia's rewrote the lyrics and everyone sang them at Julia's 80th birthday party.

Strawberry shortcake and crisp apple strudel,
Dark chocolate truffles and oodles of noodles,
Long Island duckling and peaches that cling,
These are a few of my favorite things...

I did take a risk. I said yes before I created my Julia character. But it was a calculated risk because the new character was based on characters I already had. I was 99% sure I could do Julia. I was sure inspired to try!

As I created my new character, I put myself in a position in which I was *forced* to innovate — and this is key. I was accountable because I had a deadline — the day of the telegram — and I had someone counting on me, my customer. He had actually paid in advance. I forced myself to innovate because I knew that given a choice, and being a typical human being, I would continue with the same old comfortable routine instead of innovating.

JULIA'S INNOVATIVE SPIRIT

The telegram went well. The customer was happy. I loved doing Julia so much that I created a Julia Child party entertainment package. It was more extensive than a telegram — I stayed for the whole party, served hors d'oeuvres as Julia and regaled the guests with stories of her life.

I also put together a one-hour Julia Child show for seniors at independent living centers. We sang songs about food and we had a Julia quote-a-thon. Everyone had to read out a quote from Julia in their best Julia voice.

"It's a shame to be caught up in something that doesn't absolutely make you tremble with joy."

"If you're afraid of butter, use cream."

"Drama is very important in life: You have to come on with a bang. You never want to go out with a whimper. Everything can have drama if it's done right. Even a pancake."

Saying yes to Julia allowed me to expand from a singing telegram business to a theme party business. I had no idea this would happen. I just kept saying YES!

I found it easy to say yes to Julia. She was the first famous TV chef, a pioneer, an innovator.

Julia understood the need to entertain in order to educate. Once, at a cooking demonstration in a large auditorium full of spectators, she came out on stage and immediately began

101

throwing bread rolls out into the crowd, and I mean she wound up like a major league pitcher, aiming for the back row. When the audience realized she had autographed each roll, there was much scrambling about on the floor and jumping up to try and catch each roll.

You don't have to pitch bread rolls to be innovative. You just have to say yes when you're asked to do something new. Once you say yes, you'll come up with your own innovations.

Interesting side note: a Harvard Business Review study (The Innovators DNA, 2009) revealed that the more countries a person has lived in, the more likely he or she is to deliver innovative products and processes. Julia lived in China, Sri Lanka, France and the United States. And she ate delicious meals in every country.

The study found that if managers try out even one international assignment before becoming CEO, their companies deliver stronger financial results than companies run by CEOS without such experience — roughly 7% higher market performance on average.

Bring Innovation to the Whole Company

Is "saying yes" scalable? Based on current research, it *is* scalable. A 2017 study by the *Harvard Business Review* ("Data From 3.5 Million Employees Show How Innovation Really Works") looked at data from 154 public companies and a total of more than 3.5 million employees. The study found that a large number of participants comes up with more successful ideas than a small group of smart people. The more diverse kinds of people coming up with ideas, (not just engineers and managers but sales staff, support workers and manufacturing employees) the more actionable the innovations are.

So even if you're not in a leadership role yet, you can still have influence and be a creative force within your organization.

Once everyone is thinking about ideas, the whole company will be engaged in innovation, which could make all the difference in your company's ability to compete. Here's an idea - the company could make a commitment to implement a certain number of ideas a year, say 50. Or just 10 if it's a small company.

Employees could spend 15 to 30 minutes a day writing down questions that challenge the status quo. Or hold idea lunches with disparate groups of people in different parts of the company. (These brainstorming concepts were mentioned in the *Harvard Business Review*, in the December, 2009 edition.)

SAYING NO

Saying "yes" brought me success but there came a time when I decided to say no. Sometimes you have to say no to be true to yourself and keep your spirit alive.

It was a rainy, cold night in Vancouver, British Columbia, where I started my telegram career working for other telegram companies. I got a breathless phone call from Alexis at Balloon Action. "Got a telegram for you tonight. It's an apology. The guy wants balloons, flowers, the works. He paid extra."

I said yes and found myself driving to Surrey, Vancouver's low income, high crime suburb.

The address turned out to be a room at a motel that might have been a Motel 6 in its glory days. The building was huddled behind a strip mall, with no lighting, no signage, nothing to distinguish it.

A 50-ish woman answered the door. She was about five-foot-two and thin. Permanent worry marks were etched in her forehead. No make-up.

I launched into my short intro song: "Today the one who loves you best wants you to know you're better than the rest. And here I am at his request to give to you a little zest."

She stared, uncomprehending. I explained that her husband had sent a singing telegram to make her feel special. That got a smile and an invitation to come in.

I stepped through the threshold and into their hotel room/home. The musty yellow-brown carpet had suffered too many cigarette burns and not enough cleaning attempts. There were two queen-size beds with thin bedspreads that had once been a lovely rose color, now faded to dingy pink.

Two 16 or 17-year-olds — a boy and a girl — sat on one of the beds. Their expressions were sullen. The husband sat in a chair in the corner.

I told her that her husband had chosen a beautiful old jazz standard to honor her, and launched into *It Had to Be You*. I tried not to notice the scowls on the teenagers deepening as I sang. The more I sang, the more they frowned. The wife smiled and gave her husband a look full of affection.

I handed her the balloons and flowers, and backed out the door.

SETTING MY LIMITS

Driving back to Vancouver in the rain, I wondered what kind of situation I had wandered into. The kids seemed really angry with their father. The telegram gave him bonus points with their mom and they definitely didn't like that.

It dawned on me that the husband may have sent the telegram to apologize for something seriously nasty like being unfaithful or being violent. Of course, it could have been something more innocuous like forgetting an anniversary but the kids' venomous expressions made it seem like more was going on.

My gift helped him earn forgiveness but I wasn't sure he deserved it. Maybe he did; maybe he didn't. The thing is, I didn't know.

For the first time, I realized that my gift of song could be misused. That I could manipulate emotions. And that I had the right to control who I gave my gift to. After that, I was careful not to do any more forgiveness telegrams.

We have the right to bestow our gifts on others or not, as we see fit. Work is a great place to discover our ethics and values, and to decide what we will and will not do, to take a stand. Don't worry if you don't know ahead of time what your limits are. Usually you have to be in the situation to know your limit - it's not predictable ahead of time.

Even while innovating and saying yes to break the rules, you have the right to say NO if the situation doesn't make sense. You have to be true to yourself.

INNOVATION IN SIX STEPS

Here is a useful set of actions to help your innovative juices start to flow. You can choose one or two to start and then include more steps later as time allows.

Ask yourself how you can break the rules. Think of a process at work that you'd like to change. Now write down five questions about that situation that challenge the status quo.

Say yes! Like I did to the customer who asked me to create a Julia Child character. Say yes, like I did when I walked down the hallway of my church in the gorilla costume. I was driving everyone bananas! (You don't need to do that.)

Give yourself a deadline and write down the achievable small steps that will take you to your goal, like the steps I took to create my Julia Child character.

Find someone you can be accountable to, preferably someone who is *tremendously* interested in the outcome. This could be your manager, a colleague or a friend at work.

Pinpoint something about the goal that inspires you. It should make you "tremble with joy," as Julia said. How will it benefit other people?

Ask yourself these two key questions:

How can I say YES to something new that inspires me and benefits my organization?

What is my limit? When do I say no? How do I stay true to myself?

Now go forth and innovate! Bon Appetit!

◇◇

Mardi Wareham is a spirited story-teller who delivers a rousing program designed to inspire and uplift her audiences. As CEO and chief performer at Singing Telegrams of Austin, she personifies innovation and creativity. From the first time she put on a gorilla costume, she knew she wanted to disrupt the workplace. What makes her unique is her six-step blueprint for creating innovation, illustrated with stories of singing telegram hijinks. Mardi also facilitates team building – she teaches groups of people in the corporate workplace to play ukulele. She believes everyone should experience the joy of working on a great team and she loves to help people get there. Prior to starting her innovative business, she held traditional grown-up positions in marketing in the insurance, education and nonprofit sectors. Mardi and her ukulele moved to Austin from Vancouver, Canada in 2005 and are delighted to live in the Live Music Capitol of the World.

Transforming Transactions Into Interactions™

How to increase revenue, ratings and repeat customers

Jill Raff

"Good morning. McDonald's is your kind of place, may I help you please?"

This was my first job. I was seven years old when my education in customer experience began. My parents and grandparents owned McDonald's store #150 in Ocala, Florida.

I was trained on what today we'd call, "Customer First Impression." The first contact with your customer—how you greet them—is critical, setting expectations and an everlasting impression. I grew up working in the "McDonald's family," when McDonald's was the gold standard of the restaurant industry. I was raised on Ray Kroc's philosophy of QSC & V: Quality, Service, Cleanliness and Value.

Imagine you've *chosen* to go to what used to be known as a "fast food" restaurant, now called a QSR, for Quick Service Restaurant and you find yourself standing in line, a *reeeeally* long line, and you're waiting, and waiting, and waiting. Is this familiar to you? How does it make you feel?

I went to a well-known, quickly growing, QSR franchise which had just opened in Austin. Loving them when I lived in NYC, I was *so* excited! Sadly, the only thing that was "quick" was how my excitement dwindled as the line grew out the door and I noticed that: 1. Only one to two of the four registers were open. 2. There was no real customer 'interaction' once I finally placed my order. 3. The two managers were at the end of the counter, chatting amongst themselves. As if that wasn't bad enough, one of them was even leaning against the front counter *with her back to the customers*! OMWord, I could hear Ray Kroc saying, "If you have time to lean, you have time to clean." As a customer, their actions made it clear to me that I was unappreciated. I felt like nothing more than a transaction. I also thought of how my Dad always responded to seeing lines of customers at our McDonald's. It was just the opposite.

Whenever we drove by one of our stores, my Dad would always look to see if the appropriate lights were on, there was no trash around the lot, and if he ever saw there were too many customers waiting, he'd pull in saying, "I'll be right back." Well, 20-30 minutes later, my mom, my sisters and I would be still sitting in the car. I'd go in to see where he was, and inevitably he'd be shuffling between dressing buns, working the fry station, and helping at the counter to get the customers served as quickly as possible, and always with a smile.

What I didn't know then, was that these experiences would shape my future work ethic and value of the customer. What I didn't know then was the importance of being relevant and current, illustrated by all of my Mom's clever ideas for McDonald's products and promotions long before the corporation adopted them. As a result, when my parents would see Ray Kroc at meetings, Ray Kroc would always tell my Dad, "Marshall, your wife is sure some entrepreneur." Customers are always looking for the newest trend, the next hot restaurant, fun product or unique service which will save them time, money or give them a great experience.

What I didn't know then, was how much I learned from my Dad's interactions with everyone from customers, to maintenance and yardmen, to so many people who adored him because he took time to always look them in the eye, ask about their family by name, and make them feel like they were the only person in the room.

What I've found is that many companies are in a transactional business, and it doesn't matter if you're are buying a bag of ice, a coaching program, or a house, people are treated like a transaction all the time.

Believe me, you once had customers who at some point you treated like a transaction. And that's why they *used to be* your customers.

According to the Office of Consumer Affairs, it's 6-7 times more expensive to acquire a new customer than it is to keep a current one. And on the flip side, loyal customers are worth, on average, up to 10 times as much as their first purchase. I see businesses watching their profits walk out the door as unengaged and disconnected customers.

Do any of you have a customer like that, feeling unengaged and unappreciated? Have any of your employees treated your customers like a transaction? What I've learned along the way is that even if you have *one*, it's too many. If it starts to happen more and more, we have to look within and recognize, it's not the customer. We have to look at our business honestly; look at the way we run our business, look at our people, the way they are trained, or not, and ask yourself, "How often does this happen and what is that costing me"?

Society and life have taught us to look outward for blame when a problem arises. It takes being brutally honest with oneself, ego aside, to realize that any problems start from within and at the top. Businesses complain of their customers being problematic, annoying, whiny, etc. Your customer is not the problem.

YOUR CUSTOMER PROBLEMS... ARE NOT YOUR CUSTOMER.

They are bringing their issues with them wherever they go. As businesses, we must have strategies, systems and perpetual training in place on how to handle the conflicts that arise, and Transform [those] Transactions Into Interactions™.

What we think is a 'customer problem' is really an opportunity to look closely at our company's core values and mission statement, to determine if the business is engaging with its customers by the playbook established according to those values. Turn a customer's negative experience into not only a positive one, but one from which a life-long relationship will thrive, creating a raving sales force from your customers. The by-product also enables you to reduce your marketing budget.

"IT'S JUST ONE CUSTOMER." THINK AGAIN!

You may think, "It is just one customer; we have a steady flow of customers,"...not so fast. The power of a review, be it 5 stars, 4, or 3 stars or less, is an opportunity for you to connect with your customers and show them you value them. It used to be that a person who has a positive experience tells 4-5 friends, but one who has a negative experience tells 9-12 people. Now, good or bad, true or not, with one quick post they're telling billions. We are only as good as our last single client interaction or referral.

84% of people purchase because of a referral, *even if* they don't know that referral person-ally. Ratings Rock! Will yours be "positive," "negative" or "blah?" Really, there are only 2 choices because if someone feels their dining or shopping experience was just "meh/blah," it is negative. According to Lee Resources, 80% of companies say they deliver "superior" customer service, while only 8% of people think these same companies deliver "superior" customer service. This is a huge gap and opportunity cost by not knowing what your customer is feeling and thinking. The Office of Consumer Affairs states, 96% of customers who have a bad experience will *not* tell the business. This means that only 4 in 100 customers will even tell you there's a problem, giving you the chance to make it right!

If every one of your customers were asked to write a review, what would it be? A business must stand out and be memorable in a positive way. What will that "one" customer say to billions?

CHURN. CHURN. CHURN. YOUR EMPLOYEE CHURN RATE WILL ALSO BE AN INDICATOR IN YOUR CUSTOMER CHURN RATE.

Stop the Employee Churn. Your employees are the face of your company, those that interact with your customers. If your employees are not happy, and don't feel like they're a part of something bigger, neither will your customer. Empower your employees, mine talent and ideas from within for increased productivity from a happy team. When their ideas and contributions are recognized and appreciated, they will work hard to implement what they've contributed. When there is a lack of employees vested in the success of your mission, your customers ultimately suffer.

Have your employees only learned "smile training?" What systems are used in hiring and on-boarding your staff? If none, everyone involved will feel the inconsistent chaos which will result in employee churn and lost customers. It's a double whammy. The cost of losing an employee; recruitment, rehiring, retraining, and burden on the existing team, is enormous. Your customers feel the negative impact. Your employee retention and customer experience are two sides of the same coin. Customers will feel the "revolving door" and "temporary" energy. Why would someone pay for that when there are so many choices? They won't! Oracle confirms, that 89% of customers begin business with a competitor following a poor customer experience.

With this in mind, I've developed my Proprietary 7 Pillar Process for a Customer Experience Transformation™. I'll highlight the 3 guiding principles behind it, which will increase your bottom-line quickly through creating repeat customers as your advocates, your marketing sales force: It's called P.M.I.

You may be thinking: "What does Private Mortgage Insurance have to do with my business?" But this is insurance of a different kind, the all important customer retention insurance: Positive. Memorable. Interaction.

P — POSITIVE

Businesses must create a positive feeling from the customer's experience.

Does the customer feel as good, or better, about you as when they walked in?

What specifically did you or your employee do to create that positive feeling, that connection?

Will your customer walk out with that extra *air in their step*, a smile on their face and a great feeling that without conscious thought, they aren't exactly sure why they are feeling so good? That's when you know you've created a positive lasting effect.

M — MEMORABLE

How will you and your organization be remembered?

Did your customer leave with a memorable experience?

Did their interaction with you or your employees leave a positive memorable impression once they walk out your door?

Ultimately, will those memories result in referrals and repeat business? Did you *earn* their repeat business?

I — INTERACTION

Transform your Transactions Into Interactions™

Maya Angelou said it best, "I've learned that people will forget what you said, people will forget what you did, but people will never forget how you made them feel."

Remember people are people first, and customers second. Everyone wants to be spoken to, and called by name. As Dale Carnegie stated, "Remember that a person's name is to that person the sweetest and most important sound in any language." And it's such an easy thing to do!

An interaction is *not* a transaction. Customers want to feel acknowledged, appreciated, and engaged with genuine interaction, knowing their needs and desires are prioritized, not that they are just being sold to.

Businesses must assure their customers they genuinely care and want to help resolve their problem, not so they will buy from us, but rather to show them we are all people (not just sales-people) and we want to find them a solution. We are most effective and connect with others when we show empathy- that we sincerely are grateful they chose to spend their time and money with us, concerned with their genuine need, and are coming from a place of service.

When this genuine gratitude occurs, it is precisely at this moment when there is a PIV-OTAL SHIFT: A shift from caring about whether the customer is buying something, to caring about whether their problem or need is solved; whether you've added value to their life or to their business! *This* is the shift to a human interaction from a transactional interaction.

What I've found is, the world needs more connection. In this world of ever polarizing politics, uncertainty, natural disasters and virtual relationships, we are all craving genuine, simple, kind, human interactions.

When I realized that this greater connection also creates successful profitable businesses, I became obsessed by the rewards and benefits of delivering a celebrity customer experience. Obsession is the key to success.

MAKE YOUR CUSTOMER'S EXPERIENCE YOUR OBSESSION.

According to the Oxford Dictionary, the word *obsession* means "an idea or thought that continually preoccupies or intrudes on a person's mind." Some may think this equals being neurotic, narcissistic, pathological, or even psychotic. I disagree. If it's directed toward serving and benefiting others, we all benefit. It means you believe so deeply in something, it's positive outcome and its affect on others. I believe it means you're passionate and focused. So, be obsessed. Be obsessed with your customer's experience. They have *chosen* you over others, to give their time and hard-earned money. Design the customer's experience and train your team around a culture of honoring your customer's choice to come to you over your competitor.

Extraordinary customer service is what everyone deserves. It not only makes a positive memorable experience, but through the true interactions a business has with customers as person-to-person and not salesperson-to-consumer, they are creating meaningful connections.

Become obsessed with creating a culture within your company to deliver a positive memorable interaction with your customers, so they will in turn become obsessed with doing business with you. According to the Harvard Business Review, increasing customer retention rates by a mere 5%, increases profits by 25% to 95%. Bottom line: If you're not managing *every* interaction with your customer, making it positive, making it *memorable* in a positive way, it starts to cost you your business.

What I mean by that is that organizations don't focus a lot of their internal investment on systems and training to connect with their customers. They don't have an intentional program to create a celebrity experiences on every level. So as a result, they don't have repeat customers, their employees don't really care because they're not lead to care, they then have to cut back on their business development when they should be growing.

When businesses create core values around developing relationships with each and every customer consistently, they'll see their revenues and ratings surge. Ultimately, this decreases margins, revenue & the bottom line.

DETAILS OF YOUR CUSTOMER'S PROFILE YOU'LL KNOW, THEN IN YOUR CASH WILL FLOW.

Growing up in McDonald's, I know a thing or two about the "secret sauce." The "Secret Sauce" in your business success is in the details. It is indeed the small things that make the biggest impact on your customers. They are the things that matter most when people remember their experience. Giving good "service" is the baseline expectation, the given. The service is what creates the "transaction," but there's nothing particularly special about it. Without the customer buying from you, there would be no need for employees, nor your business. It's all in how you look at the age old question: "Which came first, the chicken or the egg," or in this case, "the customer or the business offering?"

If there's nothing to make you stand out, to distinguish yourself, you're only a commodity and will be shopped by price alone. The result will be a consistent race to compete by cutting prices until you're out of business. A recent study from Capgemini states that 8 in 10 consumers are willing to pay more for a better customer experience. It's your decision: commodity or engagement?

How do we make that personal connection, learn details of what's important to your customer versus what is important to you, or what you think is important to them? Is it in your training? Is it systematized? Do you evaluate and follow up?

Recognize those important people, names, dates, celebrations in your customers' lives so you create a relationship with them. In turn, they feel a genuine connection to you, and connection = profit[TM].

When an organization builds a culture where they establish core values and hire, train, execute, evaluate and follow up based on those values, they will experience not just the classic win-win strategy, but something even deeper, more meaningful and sustaining. I propose a Winning Trifecta™: a win for the owner, employee and customer. It's the perfect synergistic cycle. This customer will be transformed into a life long customer. Their loyalty will equate to exponentially more business for you as they become your ambassadors.

I have lived around the world, spanning 3 continents, 6 countries and worked in several different markets, with customer experience always being the common thread. My diverse background gives me a distinct multi-dimensional perspective, to create customer experience strategies for my clients.

Hindsight is 20-20. What I didn't know then is April 1st, 1994 when my Dad was diagnosed with stage 4 lung cancer, that it was no April Fool's joke.

What I didn't know then, was that my Dad would rally after chemo, to attend the McDonald's convention, in order to receive their 35 year owner/operator award, one of the few at that time, and that we'd lose him only 6 months later.

What I didn't know then, was that everything I learned from my parents while growing up in McDonald's would be the foundation of my life's work and purpose, to help businesses make connections and prosper by prioritizing and elevating the customer. In this way, I am honoring my father and his legacy lives on within me.

Are you ready to stop leaving money on the table and give your business an instant revenue boost? The solution is simple: Transform your Transactions Into Interactions™. I can help you do that. I look forward to hearing about your customer experiences. Connect with me at www.jillraff.com.

Jill Raff is a creative problem solver with a keen eye and awareness to all things "customer experience". As a Customer Experience Strategist and CEO at Raff & Associates, Jill uses her deep culinary background and proficiency amongst other industries, spanning across 3 continents, to help restaurants and hospitality groups decrease their employee churn rate and increase their revenues, ratings and repeat customers. Jill developed her Proprietary Seven Pillar Process for a Customer Experience Transformation™. Her unique value is in her ability to weave strategies from across industries, cross-pollinating multiple practices otherwise not used in the single lane of one industry. Some of Jill's qualifications: McDonald's Corporation "family", Fashion Designer in renown American & European labels, Le Cordon Bleu, Paris graduate, Stagier in Harrod's Pastry Kitchen, François Payard, and Guido Ristorante 1* Michelin in Italy, NYC Food Stylist, closed $20+ Million in sales as licensed Realtor® in NY and TX.

Don't Take Anything Personally

Cheryl Jones

MR. COFFEE MAN

Late one afternoon, I was summoned to the front desk of the historic downtown hotel in which I worked. My role was Banquet Manager, which means that I oversaw meeting rooms, catered events and coffee breaks. It was unusual for me to receive a request from the front desk clerk to come to the lobby. I was puzzled, wondering what he needed.

As I walked up to the desk, the clerk pointed to a man standing only a few feet away. I stepped closer to question the clerk, hoping to gain some insight into the situation beforehand. The clerk shrugged his shoulders and cocked his head to one side, indicating that he didn't know what the man wanted. I walked over, extended my hand to introduce myself, and before I could get a word out he began yelling.

His voice boomed at such a volume that it filled the open lobby. It was so loud that it echoed off the ceiling, two-stories above. He continued yelling at me, saying things like, I didn't know what I was doing; I shouldn't be in this job; Didn't I know who he was; And he had paid good money to hold his meeting here and he expected more!

To make the situation worse, there were a dozen or so guests in the lobby who stopped what they were doing and were now transfixed by the scene. Their mouths hung open in astonishment! I felt completely humiliated, still with no idea what was wrong.

The longer he yelled, the smaller I felt — like Alice in Wonderland when she drinks the shrinking potion. As he yelled, I felt I was getting smaller and smaller. I remember standing there, not knowing how to respond, wondering what I had done to make him so angry with me.

The yelling never seemed to subside. I stood there taking the abuse, praying that someone, anyone would come to my rescue. I remember thinking, "Help, please. Someone save me from the awful man!" No one stepped in to help, not even the desk clerk. He just stood there, spell-bound by the situation.

Then I had the thought, "I could faint right here. Right here on the cold marble floor. That would make him stop yelling." But I didn't faint. (I couldn't figure out how to fake a faint without hurting myself or I might have tried it.) I even prayed that it was just a bad dream and at any moment I'd wake up at home in my bed. No, it was not a dream. It was real, darn it. As a last resort, I recall glancing over at the front desk looking for support. There were three clerks there now. They all stood there just as stunned, wide-eyed as I was. There was no support there.

The man continued to rant for several more minutes. The more he ranted, the less I heard anything he said. It was out of self-preservation that I tuned him out. Never in my career had I been treated like that by a guest. I was frozen in my tracks. I couldn't move. I felt humiliated, helpless and powerless to do anything. The worst part of the experience was that I thought that because he was the "customer," I had to take the abuse.

In the days following the lobby incident, I continued to feel beat up, abused and not as confident as I had felt before. His explosion had shaken my world – stunned and upset my self-assurance. Even though I thought that I had tuned him out, instead I had internalized every word he had said. His ugliness had caused me to second guess my ability to do my job. I found myself second guessing simple decisions. It created so much self-doubt that I was now fearful I would lose my job.

At this point of the story, you might like to know why he was so angry. His anger stemmed from a belief that the coffee on his meeting's coffee break was "old," even though, I assured him that the coffee was indeed fresh. He didn't like it and wanted it to be "fresher."

For the next two days, I avoided him at every possible intersection and instead sent the banquet captain to handle the group's needs. On the third day of their five-day meeting, the group took their afternoon break ten minutes early. This caused a crisis in the banquet depart-ment, because the coffee had not been put out on the table yet.

The banquet team had been strategically brewing the coffee later than usual to coincide with the group's break schedule so the coffee would be as fresh as possible. On that afternoon, the coffee had just finished brewing and was being placed in the urn when the group broke from their meeting — ten minutes early. There was a mad scramble by the banquet staff and myself to get the coffee up two flights of stairs, before Mr. Coffee Man blew another gasket! Until that afternoon, as a team we had succeeded in keeping him happy by supplying "fresh" coffee, which also meant it kept me from getting a verbal beating. That was all about to change. More about that in a bit.

Don't Take Anything Personally

One of the core concepts in the book, *The Four Agreements, A Toltec Wisdom Book*, by Don Miguel Ruiz is, "Don't Take Anything Personally." Ruiz says, "Nothing others do is because of you. What others say and do is a projection of their own reality, their own dream. When you are immune to the opinions and actions of others, you won't be the victim of needless suffering." This is a concept that I wish I'd firmly grasped during the interaction with Mr. Coffee Man. It might have helped influence my interpretation of his outburst.

Something that did help me rebound from the events with Mr. Coffee Man, was something I had learned while in middle school. It was an interpersonal communication theory called "Transactional Analysis" or TA. The theory breaks interpersonal interactions down into individual transactions and helps identify the mode from which each person is communicating, so that you can make an informed decision of your response instead of having a knee-jerk reaction.

The way I remember the TA theory is that it resembles a chemical reaction — add one-part chemical X to one-part chemical Y and you get a neutral reaction. However, if you were to add one-part chemical E to one-part chemical X, BOOM! You get an explosion. Communication between people can be the same way. Those BOOM reactions are the ones we would like to avoid.

Interpersonal communication is a transaction between two people, much like a reaction between two chemicals. Surely, you've heard of or seen an interaction between a customer and customer service representative where things didn't go so well. A customer who was angry about missing his flight and chooses to yell at the representative in an attempt to get what he wants. His behavior may even cause the representative to raise her voice, too. Another situation is the child who throws a tantrum in the middle of the store as the parent is loudly scolding the child not to throw a tantrum! Neither situation ever ends well. But these are great examples of how we all have the capability to show up in one of three ways — as the Parent, Child or Adult.

Coats of Interaction

Think about it this way. Each time you engage in a conversation, you have the opportunity to show up from one of three versions of yourself. We'll refer to each of the versions as putting on a coat, which means you have three coats to choose from: Parent, Child and Adult. I've chosen to use a coat analogy because coats are easy to put on and take off. The coat you choose determines the demeanor which you use to interact with the other person.

Each time you engage in a conversation, you unconsciously choose one of the three coats. Your choice of coat is based on the unconscious preconceived ideas, assumptions and beliefs you hold about the person, their position and/or the situation. If you hold an assumption that the customer service rep will be unwilling to help you get on the flight you want, then you will likely show up in one of two coats – the Parent or the Child. Without consciously knowing it, you choose the coat that you believe is best to help you reach your goal. If you think that taking on a directive, finger-pointing, somewhat aggressive style of the Parent will get you what you want, you will likely don that coat. On the other hand, if you think that you will more likely get what you want by donning the coat of a small, helpless, underpowered Child, then you may choose that coat instead.

Each coat has a unique set of features and behaviors associated with it. Some of the features associated with the Parent coat include behavior that is: critical, judgmental, authoritarian, finger pointing, directive, and pushy. You may hear phrases such as: "I want you to do this now." "Don't you do that!" "You better listen to me and do it my way."

The Child coat features behavior such as: small, helpless, whiny, cranky, fretful, irrational, tantrums and crying. You might hear someone in a Child coat say, "No! I don't want to do that." "You can't make me!" "I want it. Why can't I have it?"

The third coat, the Adult coat is quite different from either of the other two. The Adult coat's features tend to express themselves as even toned, unemotional, with clarity, logic, and as wanting to help or solve a problem. You will likely hear this person say things like: "I see what the problem is. Let see how can we get this done." "How can I be of help?" "What is standing in our way?" "I'd be glad to take on that task. When would you like to get started?"

In the millisecond that it takes for you to decide which coat you will wear, the other person in your interaction sees you, sizes you up, and decides which coat she will wear. Some of the decision comes from the natural attraction of each of the coats.

One of the most interesting parts of TA is that each style has a unique magnetic attraction to another. The Parent magically attracts the Child and vice versa, creating a push-pull dynamic. If a dialog starts out with one person in the Child coat it will attract the Parent coat in the other person.

PARENT TO CHILD INTERACTION

Here's an example of a Parent/Child interaction in the workplace. When Rachel, the collections manager, puts on her Parent coat the other girls in the office cringe. Rachel's personality and language come across as directive, condescending and pushy. The more Rachel pushes the girls to meet the target deadlines, the more they respond with child-like behaviors. "We can't get all this done by the end of the day." "I can't work that hard!" "She's asking too much." "Who does she think she is?"

CHILD TO PARENT INTERACTION

Conversely, here's an example of what happens with a Child/Parent interaction. Susan complained that there is too much work to be done. She was feeling that she can't handle the workload, because her head is aching which isn't allowing her to work at her normal fast pace. Rachel interprets Susan's complaining as "child-like" behavior, which causes her to launch further into "parent-like" behavior by telling her that she *will* get it done by the end of the day.

PARENT TO PARENT INTERACTION

One kind of exchange that we have not talked about is the Parent to Parent exchange. You may have participated in or been a witness to this kind of interaction. If you have, you know that this kind of interaction isn't pretty.

While working with the customer service employees at an Arena facility, I learned of a group the Arena hosted annually that epitomized Parent to Parent interaction. These were the parents of those children involved in competitive cheerleading.

Competitive cheerleading consists of girls and boys, ages 5 to college-age who compete with other cheerleading teams across the state or nation, performing routines and gymnastic stunts. According to the Arena employees, cheer-parents were known to be some of the most demanding and aggressive-toward-other-parents groups the employees had ever seen. The employees shared stories of how parents argued and fought with rival team parents over everything from setup and practice space to refreshments.

ADULT TO ADULT INTERACTION

The most effective, efficient and desirable method of interaction is through the Adult coat. When both parties interact from the Adult coat perspective, it eliminates the drama associated with the other styles. There is no need for struggle, and communication is clear.

Now, take a moment to think of an interaction where things didn't go the way you would have liked. As you think about that interaction, what coat were you wearing? What coat was the other person wearing? Were they similar coats? Opposites?

Most people have never heard of Transactional Analysis or the "coats of interaction," and are therefore unaware of how a chosen coat can interfere with our interactions with others. Instead, we assume that the reason there is a problem is the other person's behavior, lack of action, or bad attitude. In reality, the other person may be mirroring the complementary response coat to the coat they saw us wearing.

How can we change the coats we have chosen? How can we drop the uncooperative Parent or Child coat and adopt the cooperative coat of the Adult?

To achieve a positive outcome to just about any interpersonal communication, you must first recognize which coat you are entering the interaction with. Notice your thoughts. Notice the assumptions or beliefs you hold about the other person. Did the person's previous behavior with someone else cause you to adopt a particular point of view? Or are you feeling small, out of control, helpless or put-upon? Is someone asking too much of you and you just don't feel up to the challenge? Once you recognize the language of the coat you are wearing, you will have the power to choose differently. Using the language and behaviors of the Adult coat, you will win the respect and support of the other person in your interaction.

Reflecting on Don Miguel Ruiz's message of, "What people do or say has very little to do with you. It is a projection of their reality," reminds me that Mr. Coffee Man had his own reality. His reality may have been that he didn't like our brand of coffee. Or maybe he was trying to impress the people who were attending his meeting. Maybe he felt they were not impressed and therefore reflected poorly on him. Who knows what was going on within his reality. I know that day in the lobby was a tough reality for me.

Mr. Coffee Man Returns

When we left the story about Mr. Coffee Man, we had been successful in getting him "fresh coffee" until day three, when his group broke from their meeting 10 minutes early. As the banquet captain and I scrambled up the stairs, the men were standing in the hallway helping themselves to the snacks for the afternoon break. We placed the coffee urn on the stand and I stepped away as the captain lit the Sterno can beneath it. Mr. Coffee Man was nowhere to be seen. I breathed a sigh of relief and went back to my office to finish preparing schedules for the next day.

Late that same afternoon, after the meetings had all ended for the day, I passed by Mr. Coffee Man's meeting room. He saw me and followed me out in to hallway.

Immediately, he was standing over me, pointing his finger and yelling, once again. He demanded to know why the coffee was late on his break. I raised my hand to get his attention. Then I raised my voice so I could be heard and said, "I understand. But yelling at me is not making me want to help you." He quieted down and started speaking in a normal tone of voice. We discussed the facts and he agreed that it was not our fault that the coffee was not out when the break started.

Up until that point, Mr. Coffee Man had been donning his Parent coat all week, which continued to attract the Child in me...the Child that wanted to avoid getting in trouble. Once I moved out of the Child and into the Adult coat, by telling him that I wanted to help, but he was making it difficult, he shifted into his Adult coat, too. He couldn't stay in the Parent for long if I wasn't playing the opposing part of the Child.

As horrible and challenging as the events were with Mr. Coffee Man, they were also an excellent lesson in recognizing that you always have choices in what you are going to wear and by consciously choosing the Adult coat you will be more likely to end up with a positive outcome.

Two important things I've learned from those events are:

1. As often as possible, play in your Adult coat.

2. Don't take anything anyone does or says personally.

As an expert in personal growth and interpersonal communication, Cheryl Jones delivers interactive and fun presentations that leave her audiences more knowledgeable than when they arrived. Her ability to share breakthrough communication techniques, build healthy workplace relationships, and teach how to master personal happiness have placed her in high demand. For more than 20 years, she has surprised a variety of audiences with her ability to intuitively speak to the needs of those present. Be it through her humor or sharing of a personal story, either way, audiences relate easily and quickly to her experiences, challenges and lessons learned. The relationships and transformation she helps build in service to others is what brings her the most joy. Cheryl considers herself to be a naturalized Texan. She is married to her college sweetheart, Marvin and they live in San Antonio with their two sons, and two Shih Tzu's.

Success Over Obstacles

Lisa Walker, Ph.D.

If you've ever had the experience of feeling stuck, feeling like something is holding you back or blocking your path, preventing you from accomplishing your goals, you know how crippling that can be. Whether the obstacles arise from our past, or from the work we do, relationships, or any other life circumstance, obstacles can seem daunting enough to stop us in our tracts or even derail our plans. If we let them.

I have discovered that whatever the obstacles we face in life, what determines if we succeed or fail is our approach to these challenges. Those who succeed do so because they have goals, believe they can accomplish their goals and support that belief with the necessary actions to overcome those obstacles. Those who fail lack the awareness that they can be overcomers.

I have also discovered that successful people, those who push through challenges and accomplish their goals, operate with a framework that supports the can-do attitude. This approach allows them to plow through, jump over, get around, get under and harness whatever gets in the way of their success. Successful people leverage the very obstacles they face and use them to their advantage to produce the results they want in business and life. The key is understanding the nature of the challenge you are facing and consistently using the framework that guarantees success.

Obstacles come in all shapes and sizes and what is truly fascinating, is that once you understand the kind of obstacle you face, and have clarity on how to deal with it, then follow through with the actions you need to take, success is pretty much guaranteed.

I was only nine years old when I came face to face with an obstacle so huge, that what I did or didn't do would determine how my life would turn out as an adult. I was born in rural Jamaica to a single mother who, overwhelmed by the gravity of raising a child on her own, did the unthinkable and at three months old, she left me with a nanny and then informed her family that I had died. She never returned. My nanny became my mom, and her mother, Granny, became the love of my life. Granny raised me while mom worked hard in America to provide for her other kids and me.

Growing up in Jamaica in the seventies, one had to take an entrance examination to gain admission to one of the few high schools we had back them. Our high schools were exceptional, but with a limited number of schools, only a small number of children could attend. My dream at age nine was to be one of those kids who made it to St. Mary's High School. I knew that the only way for me to get out of Charlestown, my little rural community, and "become somebody," was to get into high school, graduate and then go to college to become a doctor. I talked incessantly about the exam to anyone who would listen. High school was not a rite of passage for every child in Jamaica at that time. Those fortunate enough to sit and pass the exam were guaranteed a coveted spot in the limited number of high schools. I had a burning desire to be one of those kids.

Students had to register for the Common Entrance Exam and each child needed to have their birth certificate to do so. No exception. I had an enormous problem. I did not have a birth certificate! In fact, it was not known if I was even registered at birth. And to make matters worse, only my birth mother's name was known, and no one knew the name of my father. The situation was further complicated by the fact that the date I celebrated as my birthday was a guesstimate. I was born in December, but the actual birthday was anybody's guess.

Granny had always told me that I was smart and destined for great things. She made me feel as if I could do anything I dreamt I could do. I believed her and still do today. So, when Granny got sick with only a couple of weeks left to register for the exam, and with no birth certificate in hand and no other adult to help me, I knew I had to get my birth certificate by myself. Going to get it by myself was a daunting task, but I was determined to make it happen. Fueled by my excitement about taking the exam and getting into high school, I was oblivious to the reality of what it would take for me to actually achieve this goal.

The Registrar's office, the office issuing birth certificates was in Spanish Town, over sixty miles from my hometown of Charlestown. The thought of traveling to Spanish Town was like going to Mars! It was the Big Event. Since Granny was sick and no other adult was available, I had to travel by myself on a rickety old country bus. I had never gone that far by myself, so I was not sure what to expect. Granny gave me just enough money for bus fare, birth certificate fees, a beef patty and soda for lunch and candy for the ride back home. I was all set.

I left home very early that morning and walked about two miles to the bus stop. When I got on the bus, it was already full, and I quickly realized that I was not going get a seat. I would have to stand. I stretched my wiry little body and held on to a rail for dear life.

The bus kept stopping to pick up more and more people, and it kept getting fuller and fuller. Since I had absolutely no idea how long it would take to get to Spanish Town, I also had no idea how many more times the bus would stop to pick up passengers. When I thought the bus truly could not take anyone else, to my horror it stopped for two women with some humongous bags. They were stacked right next to me. As the bus swerved around the winding roads, twisting and turning to avoid potholes and oncoming vehicles, I felt my body bend and stretch like a rubber band. Other times I felt pinned between adult bodies that felt like concrete one second and moist sponges the next. The smells emanating from the warm bodies, the diesel engine, and the muggy morning air made me want to faint just to get away from it all.

Despite the torture of a bus ride, I was on a mission. With each moment of panic, I reminded myself why I was on that bus. My goal was getting my birth certificate so that I could take the Common Entrance Exam. We finally arrived in Spanish Town, after what seemed like an eternity. Granny had told me the bus always stopped right across from the Registrar's Office, and she also said to let the bus driver know that's where I needed to get off, which I had done as soon as I got on the bus. With all the stops I was sure he had forgotten, but he hadn't. Just before he pulled up to the building, he yelled, "Next stop Registrar!" That was my stop, and it was time to get off.

As I got off the bus, I felt exhausted and disoriented from the roller coaster ride. My heart was racing, and I was filled with excitement at the sight of this monster of a building. The ordeal at the Registrar's Office was even scarier than riding the rickety old bus into the city. After waiting for what seemed like a lifetime for my turn with the clerk, I was finally able to give her my information and let her know that I was there to get my birth certificate. I told her my name, birth date, my birth mother's name, and the only thing I knew about my birth father, his surname.

The assumption was that his name must have been Meikle since that was my last name. Not knowing any better, I felt I had given her a lot to work with, and she would be out with my long-awaited birth certificate in a flash. That was not the case. She searched and searched and could not find a birth certificate for Lisa Meikle. It was now late afternoon, and she had gone on to look up birth certificates for other people. She told me she would get back to me later since she couldn't spend so much time on my case with so many others waiting. My heart was racing the whole time. What if I missed the bus? What if she couldn't find it? What if I didn't get to go to high school after all? I was so terrified I could hardly eat the patty and soda I bought for my lunch.

The bus was due to return sometime close to five in the evening. It was now after four, and I still had no birth certificate. I was terrified! The clerk told me that if she didn't find it, I could always come back another day with an adult who could provide her with more information. But I knew that was not going to happen. Granny was sick, and the Common Entrance exam was only a couple of weeks away, and I was taking it. I could hear Granny's voice in my head telling me that I would get my birth certificate and that I would take the exam, come hell or high water. The confidence in her voice inside my head reassured me, and though I was still terrified, I believed my Granny that I would overcome this obstacle.

By their very nature, obstacles challenge us to change, adapt and grow.

Obstacles push us out of our comfort zone and cause us to think and act in ways we may not have even thought of before. Obstacles can help us get rid of old habits that sabotage our work; they can help us develop new ways of seeing ourselves in the world and seeing the impact we have and can continue to have on the world. Obstacles can be teachers if we let them. Knowing the facts about the obstacles we face, the ones that seem to stop us dead in our tracks, block our path, threatening to ruin our hard work and compel us to hit the pause button and think, helps us understand the significance they have in our life. So rather than seeing obstacles as something working against us, we can see them as the path to fulfilling our goals.

LIFE IS AN OBSTACLE COURSE.

Have you ever noticed that once you begin to think of embarking on a new adventure, you also notice obstacles you've never seen or thought of before? That's the thing with obstacles; they creep up once we begin to get serious about making significant changes in our life. They cause us to slow down, doubt ourselves, question our vision and pull us back into old patterns of thinking and behavior that will prevent us from making progress. But that's if we let them. When we harness the power of our obstacles, we can use the pause they create to reflect and work through unresolved issues, dismantle limiting ways of thinking, discard outdated mindset and create the space for a more powerful self to emerge. Facing obstacles and pushing through them prepares us to be more fully present and ready for the growth we are about to experience.

I have discovered that the secret to overcoming obstacles is learning how to leverage them to our advantage. We will always have things to delay us, stop us, or cause a detour on our journey to accomplishing our goals. The key is recognizing that every challenge we face has a reason for showing up in our life. A massive wall keeps us out of dangerous places and can also provide the opportunity to learn how to use a ladder. Seeing the reason behind the obstacle allows us to see the possibility it brings when harnessed to our advantage. We may uncover something new about ourselves, find a better way to manage a task, or develop skills that open new avenues to make an impact on others.

Obstacles may also cause you to assess a situation, person or thing, reconsider our approach, and can even cause us to change course. When we allow ourselves to rethink, and to listen to the messages we receive, we'll find we are led in the direction that gives us the best results for the situation. A river running its course must seep, swirl and snake around corners, erode banks, tumble over boulders and pick up speed before emerging as a magnificent force of power in the form of a mighty waterfall. So too, the very forces that slow us down, create barriers or crash into us can help us find our power.

What Kind of Obstacle are You Facing?

While we face many external obstacles such as racial and political tensions and wars that threaten to tear people apart, most of our obstacles are internal. We face challenges at work, in our relationships; we face pain, grief, loss, and frustration that can at times feel crippling. The obstacles can be mental, emotional, physical or even just perceived. They come in all shapes and sizes and identifying the kind of obstacle helps us learn how to deal with it effectively. The more we understand our obstacles and their purpose in our lives, the more prepared we are to turn them into opportunities.

Turning Obstacles into Opportunities

We place ourselves at a great advantage when we embrace the attitude that obstacles are opportunities to stretch us and test us, to push us to try new things, and ultimately to help us grow and succeed. The process starts with considering the outcome we desire. I wanted desperately to take the Common Entrance Exam as that was my only ticket to high school, college, and ultimately to the career and life I wanted. Once I was clear on what I wanted, that clarity fueled my desire and allowed me to adapt and cultivate a specific way of thinking about how I was going to accomplish my goal.

I knew I had to do whatever it would take for me to get my birth certificate. So even though I was scared to death about going to Spanish Town by myself, my burning desire to take the exam and get into high school, was stronger than any fear that gripped my mind. My mind-set was that I had to get this done no matter what. So, I was clear on what I wanted and why I wanted it. What was left was the how. How will I overcome the obstacle? What specific steps do I need to take? Who will help me? What resources will I need?

At this point, I had done everything a nine-year-old child could do to secure her birth certificate. I sat peering in the back of this enormous room, watching every move of the clerk searching for my birth certificate. My stomach was in knots; I was on pins and needles, waiting for some sign, any sign that she had found something. We were down to the wire as the bus could come at any minute now. After much shuffling in the back, pouring through big brown folders, the lady came out with a piece of paper in her hand and a smile on her face.

I leaped off the chair as if someone had given me an electric shock. And before she could even call my name, I was at the counter, ready for the good news. She presented the piece of paper to me and said, "I think I found your birth certificate." I was sure she had found it. She explained that it was hard to find because I had my mother's last name wrong, and the filing was done in her name. To complicate matters, the birth date I had given her was not my real birth date. Instead of December 15, I was actually born on December 8th. None of that mattered to me at all. What mattered was the fact that in my hand, I held the key to my future. I was on cloud nine! I was so excited I could hardly contain myself. The ride back home on the hot, packed, smelly, rickety old bus was sheer joy.

I knew Granny would be proud of me. She would always, "You are so smart," "You can do anything you put your mind to." I now felt I had proved that I was smart and that I could do great things. Getting my birth certificate was one of those great things. Granny gave me reasons to make me believe I could do great things. She gave me the love, support, encouragement, and resources to face my obstacles, to push through and use them for my good. Through study and practice, I have expanded on the basic framework Granny gave me for approaching life's challenges.

At the core when faced with an obstacle, my reflexive action is to first think of the result I want, analyze the obstacle, then figure out my plan of action and follow through. You may not have Granny's voice in your head as I do; you do, however, have this framework that helps you focus on your burning desire, maintain an optimistic can-do attitude and get to work doing what you must, to accomplish your goals. Overcoming obstacles is a discipline that, when practiced with conviction, leads to triumph.

Lisa Walker, Ph.D. is a psychologist, executive coach, speaker, relationship strategist, mediator and facilitator of difficult conversations. Dr. Walker is coach and advisor to leaders across industries. She served on the faculty of the University of Texas at Austin and is a Mentor for The IC² Institute, an interdisciplinary research unit of The University of Texas at Austin which works to advance the theory and practice of entrepreneurial wealth creation. She works with leaders to push through obstacles, improve themselves, build positive work relationships and boost productivity. Her specialties include customized presentations and training program for developing strong leaders, building positive workplace relationships, personalized coaching plans to assist in determining and achieving goals, as well as customized support for corporate initiatives for maximizing success. Dr. Walker uses the power of emotional intelligence, neuroscience, and mindfulness to create and nurture resonant relationships.

Quality over Quantity:
Strategies for Becoming a
More Intentional & Successful Networker

An excerpt from *The Intentional Networker:*
Attracting Powerful Relationships, Referrals & Results in Business

By Patti DeNucci

In planning for the coming year, Ethan worked on creating a weekly scheduling template. He was particularly interested in seeing how much time he should set aside for coffee and lunch dates, networking luncheons, and other social, professional, and business development events. He glanced with satisfaction at his large database of contacts, which included a huge array of friends, colleagues, clients, possible venture partners, referral sources, advisors, vendors, professional contacts, prospects, and others – almost everyone from whom he had received a business card in the last five years. In addition, Ethan had a stack of business cards he'd accumulated from recent networking events. These were new contacts he wanted to know better, many of whom had invited him to meet and visit over coffee or lunch. Ethan felt extremely popular!

A devoted networker and a firm believer in the power of connections, Ethan enjoyed building relationships. He was a people person and most of his business came from referrals. But as he did some quick math he experienced a paradigm shift.

Ethan noted that he typically worked forty-eight weeks out of the year and devoted an average of forty to forty-five hours a week to his business activities, including time with clients, marketing activities, and administrative projects. This schedule gave him time for some writing, his family, and training for a triathlon, which was a passion for him.

128

As Ethan made his calculations, he discovered that if he hoped to have even one phone chat, coffee, or lunch with each contact in his database plus attend one or two networking or association events a week, he'd be spending *all* his working hours on the phone, at coffee, at lunch, or out of the office. It was clear he'd need to double the hours in his work week if he had any chance of keeping up with his networking schedule, handling projects from his existing list of clients and tending to other business tasks.

This was not acceptable to Ethan. He did not want to give up the time with his kids, his writing, or his athletic training. Additionally, he was not in a position to add more staff or expand his marketing budget.

The light went on for Ethan. He realized he needed to become more focused and selective concerning where he invested his energies and time. He realized that he must figure out which clients, contacts, networking efforts, professional memberships, and commitments created the most profitable and satisfying results and value for him and his business. To do that, he needed to know what characteristics these valuable contacts shared, and how to focus on and attract them and only them.

Ethan's planning suddenly addressed different issues, such as how to focus his time, energy, and resources, and how to develop a method that would help him become more discerning and disciplined. He saw that there could be a downside to having too many contacts in his database, which had grown too large to manage. He had reached his CCM (Connections Critical Mass). It was suddenly clear to him that more is not always better.

Like other enthusiastic networkers and extroverts, Ethan had believed everyone he met and every business function he attended had something to offer him and his business. His open-ended, open-minded approach may have been a great way to take his first steps when his business was young and his database small, but things were different now. As his business matured and his database and networking calendar grew, they were on the verge of robbing him and his business of valuable time, resources, and energy.

Ethan's phone was ringing and his email inbox was always full. Both of these situations could be perceived as signs of a healthy business. However, more of these calls and emails were just "connections clutter": invitations to sales events and fundraisers from people he hardly knew, requests to have lunch or coffee from contacts who wanted his time, energy, or advice (usually for free), requests from prospects who desired his services and expertise, but had K-Mart budgets or could only pay him on spec. Ethan was also being invited to serve on committees, write and contribute articles, and speak at or emcee events. Some of these were potentially excellent opportunities, but many were requests for Ethan's time and expertise, often without any compensation.

It was all becoming overwhelming. Things had to change.

Note this wasn't about Ethan becoming a snob or acting like he was better than anyone else. It simply meant it was time for him to move to another level of discipline and focus. He finally saw that as a small business owner he had a finite amount of time to work and connect.

Analyze who and what is right for you and your business or career.

Does Ethan's story sound familiar? If you're like Ethan and find yourself swamped by an unwieldy database, an overactive networking schedule, and an increased demand for your time and expertise without sufficient return or compensation, here are some steps you can take to become more focused on quality and results. The methods described here are a great way to reach greater clarity on what feeds you and your business, so you can:

- Focus.
- Invest your time, energy, and resources wisely.
- Attract and build worthwhile relationships.
- Move to a new level of efficiency, productivity, discernment, and results.

Start with the 80:20 Rule.

Also known as the Pareto Principle, the 80:20 Rule states that typically 80% of most results come from 20% of the causes. For example, you probably wear 20% of the clothes in your closet 80% of the time. Or you may use 20% of the ingredients in your cupboard, pantry, or refrigerator in 80% of your meals. And you probably spend 80% of your time with 20% of your friends.

You can apply the 80:20 Rule in a multitude of ways to figure out what quality means to you and your business. Ask yourself:

Which 20% of your:

- Clients
- Contacts
- Friendships

- Associations/Memberships

- Networking events

- Coffees, lunches & happy hours

Bring you 80% of your:

- Profits, most rewarding projects, and testimonials

- Referrals, ideas, tips, news, and valuable opportunities

- Clients, connections, and news on best practices

- Enjoyment, energy, inspiration, and support

Put the 80:20 Rule to use in as many ways to analyze as many situations as you can think of. You will gain a profound new perspective on the value of just about every relationship you have and every activity into which you put time, energy, and resources.

From there, you can learn to recognize the traits of the people and opportunities that have the highest potential to be your Top Customers and Contacts (a.k.a. Twenty Percenters or Top 20%) from the get-go. This will enable you to energize yourself and your business rather than to deplete it.

It's not always about money.

I have several colleagues who are not clients of mine, nor am I a client of theirs. Money is neither mentioned nor exchanged except when we are debating whose turn it is to pick up the lunch tab. Yet we exchange priceless information and solve many business dilemmas when we put our heads together. We are each other's loyal and trusting advisors. People like this can be among your most valuable business allies and assets, so don't discount them just because you didn't make a monetary profit from your association with them.

Likewise, treasure your best, most encouraging friends. They may fit into your top 20% because you simply enjoy being around them. You sparkle in their presence. You pick up the phone when you see their number on caller ID and are always eager to see them. They inspire and energize you. They support and appreciate you and find every opportunity to let you know it. They give you honest feedback when you need a fresh perspective. There is value in this level of friendship. Through thick and thin, we all need these close relationships to keep going.

It's also important to feel the satisfaction of giving back. Giving to others can bring you value if you choose your pro bono projects, volunteer commitments, and leadership contributions wisely. For example, you may find it energizing to mentor someone who is eager to hear and act on your guidance; someone who you can watch blossom into an amazing leader. And it may be worthwhile on many levels to volunteer your time to a professional association or non-profit organization or to speak pro bono before a group. You can learn new skills and demonstrate those you already have. There can be plenty of value here.

Define and document the profile of your Top 20%

Now that you have an idea as to the Top 20% in your database who bring you 80% of your business or other positive results, it's time to figure out what qualities or characteristics these high-value, high performing clients, contacts, advisors, friends, events, commitments, and appointments share. You may note some patterns here as well.

This is an important step as it helps you define and identify what "quality" means to you and your business. It also will make it easier for you to tune your "radar" to spotting certain traits in people and events down the road, thus helping you recognize potential Twenty Percenters more readily when you're ready to seek more of them.

Analyze the connection.

How, where, and under what circumstances did you initially connect with the person or opportunity? Did they meet you as a result of a talk you gave at a luncheon or an article you wrote for the local business journal? Did you meet on an airplane or at a workshop or cocktail party? Did someone refer or introduce you or somehow create the circumstances of your meeting? The more you can remember and record about how you met the better.

For example, let's say Mary Jones is your best client. You met her through your colleague John Anderson. You and John used to work together at Company XYZ. You heard about your job at Company XYZ via Ann Smith who you met at a networking event given by an association you belong to. You get the idea.

Dig down into the layers of circumstances, names, places, and events that brought you your best clients, colleagues, and opportunities. Document them; they hold clues as to who and what works best to bring you the most fortunate contacts, connections, and circumstances.

Describe the characteristics of your Top 20%.

Come up with descriptive words and phrases to describe the characteristics of your most valuable clients and contacts. These words and phrases help you define what you are attracted to, what "quality" means for you, and ultimately what results in good fortune for you and your business.

You will start to notice patterns that reveal what quality and value mean to you. This new awareness will make it much easier for you to recognize what fits into your world and what doesn't, which is equally valuable.

Develop your unique set of criteria.

Come up with a list of questions to ask yourself about people, situations, and events, as well as how you make decisions about them. These can further help you document the characteristics valuable in your work and life.

Here are some examples:

Does this person/organization/product/service/event/resource:

- **Bring something positive and worthwhile to you or your organization in terms of revenue, referrals, support, expertise, energy, or enjoyment?**
- **Value, align with, or in some way compliment your expertise, time, and skills?**
- **Reflect well on you and your organization?**
- **Believe in and actively support "win-win" situations?**
- **Follow a code or set of values that align with yours?**
- **Participate in the ebb and flow and development of the relationship?**
- **Help you propel your business, projects, dreams, and goals forward?**

Try this!

Apply "The Energy Test." This is an elegantly simple way to measure who or what is a good fit for you. Simply note how you feel after you've interacted with a person or client, attended an event, participated in a program, served on a board, or spent time on a project. Was the experience energizing, depleting, or neither? Make a note about this on your calendar or schedule or list the interactions in a notebook. Use a plus (+) for the energizers, a zero (0) for the so-sos, and a minus (-) for the negatives. Strive for nothing less than all "+'s."

Sure, no relationship is perfect, and no client, project, group, event, or commitment is *always* going to be energizing, but you'll quickly begin to see patterns. Use this information to make decisions on whether or not to schedule or attract more of the same.

And remember that everything is subject to change. What was once energizing may no longer be so. Check in with your feelings, attitude, and energy levels. Make adjustments accordingly.

CREATE YOUR TOP CONTACT LIST

When you become aware of and accustomed to evaluating who and what is best for you and your business, take a next step that further refines your Top 20%: create a list of your Top 10, 25, 50, or even 100 or 150 contacts, clients, projects, colleagues, associations, or obligations. These can help you hone in on where you want to devote most of your time and energy.

Just like the clothing items that are the favorites in your wardrobe, these are your favorites in your database. They are your Inner Circle or even your Board of Advisors. Who would you put on this list, and why? Understand that the list will probably evolve over time. Create systems for keeping actively in touch and engaged with these.

Though you will focus on your Top 20%, devoting time for meetings, calls, and personal notes, find and implement creative ways to stay in touch with the masses – and to meet new people, make new contacts. Efficient ways to stay in touch with many people can involve email and social media. Use these thoughtfully and strategically.

Focusing your Top 20% is not about being elitist; it's about focusing on what is right for you and what helps you stay energized and "fed" so you can continue to be productive and create the best results for you, your career, or your business.

WHY TO DO THIS WORK?

As you become a seeker of quality, you and your brand become associated with quality. Why? Because your choices and associations reflect who you are, what you're all about, what's important to you, and what you want. You gain credibility for your focus, authenticity, discernment, and integrity. You demonstrate that you are selective, and that you have high standards. Others notice this and the ones who matter will appreciate it.

Being selective is an indicator that you are purposeful, serious about quality, and exercise good judgment. It helps solidify your reputation, builds trust, and brings you increased power to attract more good people — and even more good fortune. Smart successful people generally want to do business with other smart and successful people.

As you become more intentional, you will likely discover that some people and activities are no longer a fit for you. You can no longer expend the energy on them. That is part of growth and change, for them and for you.

Are you upholding the same standards that will earn you a spot on others' Top 20% List?

As a final note, always hold yourself to the same high standards you set for others. As you analyze what you want and need, don't forget to do some self-examination as well. Regularly and honestly consider whether you are living up to the high standards to which you are holding others. What are you doing to create relationships that are mutually beneficial?

What are you doing to earn your spot in the Top 20% of those you work with, admire, and receive value from?

Are you a Twenty-Percenter with your 20%? This is a key component to being in integrity with yourself and others. As you scrutinize others, expect that they will do the same with you.

_____

Want to discover more strategies and tips like the ones found in this segment of Patti's award-winning book, *The Intentional Networker: Attracting Powerful Relationships, Referrals & Results in Business*? There are eight more chapters you just might find invaluable. The book is available on Amazon and via other online retailers.

Patti DeNucci is a conference and corporate speaker, workshop facilitator, and award-winning author. She works with motivated people who are ready to Live, Work & Connect at a Higher Level™. Her clients have included Microsoft, Dell, HP, BazaarVoice, Rodan + Fields, Texas Conference for Women, PayPal, LoneStarOvernight (LSO), Silicon Valley Bank Private Equity, and many others. Patti is a member of the National Speakers Association as well as past president of the Austin Chapter and an alumni of NSA's Chapter Leadership Committee. For more details, please visit Patti's website at www.intentionalnetworker.com or contact her at patti@intentionalnetworker.com

How to Survive Caregiving

Jim Comer

On the morning of February 20, 1996, I lived in Los Angeles, had a good job with excellent benefits, enjoyed a caring group of friends and sang in the church choir. I had been in California for 13 years and thought my life was stable.

I was mistaken.

At 7 a.m. my phone rang and I heard the voice of Lisa Huff, my parents' next-door neighbor in Dallas. In 34 years she had never called me. I braced myself for bad news, and she delivered it.

Lisa told me that my dad was walking up and down in front of the house as if he was in a trance. She thought he was having a stroke. Lisa's sidewalk diagnosis proved correct. Caring for my mother, who had early Alzheimer's, had taken its toll on my 86-year-old father. Within hours he was in intensive care, I was on a plane to Dallas, and my world changed forever. At age 51, I became a "parent" for the first time. Mine was not a planned parenthood.

When I walked into the hospital room, I could hear my parents' friends breathe a collective sigh of relief. The only child, the surviving son, was back. The man with all the answers had arrived! If only that had been true: I didn't even know the questions. Now it was too late for the conversations we never had. Dad couldn't walk or talk, and had no control of his bodily functions. Mother was confused, unsure of what had turned our lives upside down.

It was time for me to take charge, but I didn't have the basic information I needed. During my twice-yearly trips home, Dad and I talked about "important" things like the Dallas Cow-

136

boys or who should be elected president. I knew how he stood on the federal deficit but had no idea about his own investments.

Each time I mentioned the possibility of them selling the house and moving closer to our relatives in Central Texas, Dad would get up and walk out of the room. And I let him get by with that year after year. Instead of confronting my dad and demanding that we have a conversation, I remained a polite Texas son, he stayed in denial, and we talked about football instead of the future.

Suggestions on Having the Talk I Never Had

Bite the bullet, gather your siblings — even if some are on Skype — and talk to your parents about what they want and don't want as they age. Having this conversation may be a uncomfortable at first, but so was their attempt to tell you about sex.

Don't sidestep hard topics. Good caregiving is not about avoiding issues, but facing them. Be sure to have someone take notes or record the conversation.

Find out which siblings are going to be active caregivers, who will send money but not show up often, and who will be missing in action.

Make sure that your parents have an up-to-date will and that you know where it's kept. Seven out of ten Americans do not have a will. Ten out of ten will die. I know because I Googled it.

Listen more than you talk.

Give your parents the respect and dignity they deserve, even if you disagree with their plans—or lack of them.

Depending on the state of their health, don't try to make big decisions in the first meeting. This talk should begin an ongoing conversation.

Congratulate yourself for getting the subject on the table, no matter how the conversation goes.

Suddenly faced with making scores of decisions, I had to start from scratch. I had never seen their wills, powers of attorney, or the contents of the lock box at their bank. I knew little about their finances - other than how much they'd lent me - and nothing about their insurance. It turns out they were insured for everything except long-term care.

As the surviving brother and only child since 1970, I became the designated decision maker. The hospital staff made it clear that I would need to find a rehabilitation center within one week.

I knew it couldn't be in Dallas because we had no family there. Our relatives were in Central Texas. When there is a medical crisis, friends and neighbors are helpful, but family is essential.

I flew to Austin in a rain-storm and visited four rehab centers in one day. They all looked the same to me. I chose St. David's because a nurse smiled at me. I needed a smile badly that day and prayed that her kindness would be reflected in the care my dad received.

Mother flatly refused to leave Dallas as she didn't understand that she could no longer live alone. My cousins, assuring their eventual sainthood, agreed to care for her while I tried to figure out what to do. But first I had to get her to Austin. To deal with this dilemma, I came up with a tactic I called, "therapeutic lying."

The night before we had to leave, I packed for my mother. The next morning, I asked innocently, "Mama, would you like to go get some ice cream?" Mother never turns down ice cream, not even at 8:30 on Monday morning. She smiled, put down her coffee cup, got into the car and we drove away from her home of 34 years. She never saw it again.

I stopped at the first Dairy Queen we came to and bought her the biggest, gooiest chocolate sundae imaginable, but somewhere around Waco she must have realized we were going on a longer ride. When we got to my cousins' house, I kissed her goodbye, headed for the airport and jumped on a plane for LA. My body went back to work the next day, but my mind remained in Texas.

For six months, I flew into Austin every other weekend. The first time I visited the rehab center, I found Dad alone in his room. He was unable to walk, make sentences or control his bodily functions. But his vision was good and his mind was alert. He gathered his strength and forced out three words: "Get...me...pills." He was not talking about aspirin. He wanted me to get pills so he could end his life. No one had prepared me for this moment. As he was nearly deaf, I had to yell my response. "Dad, I can't do that, I'll go to jail!...Not hell, Dad, jail!...Well, maybe hell, too! I can't do it."

He was not pleased with my response. Later that day, one of his doctors suggested an operation on his prostate that might restore bodily functions. It worked, and within two weeks Dad was using the restroom on his own. That's when he decided he wanted to live.

Foolishly, I thought things might calm down. Wrong. For the first time, I experienced "parent-teacher" calls. They were not about why Johnny can't read, but why John Comer was raising so much hell on the fourth floor. Bending the truth once again, I told exasperated social workers that I would talk to my father. Fat chance. With his hearing loss, Dad could not hear my long-distance pleas not to yell at the nurses. Just when he decided to get with the program, St. David's kicked him out for bad behavior. I had one week to find a new facility.

The next Friday I flew into Austin and headed for the only long-term-care community in town that offered both assisted living for mother and rehab for dad. I told the Admissions Director I needed to move my parents in on Monday, an impossible request. She didn't look hopeful, but checked their availability and suddenly broke into a grin. Amazingly, they had two openings on Monday.

Even with my parents in the same community, I found myself unable to keep up with their constantly changing needs. Finally, I realized I couldn't do what needed to be done from more than a thousand miles. I had to make a choice: move my folks to California where they knew only me and things were much more expensive, or quit my job and move back to Texas where I had not lived in 30 years. I chose to parent my parents and never regretted it.

I quit my job, sold most of my furniture, rented a U-Haul, and moved back to Texas. Becoming a caregiver was not easy. I had to learn the language of Medicare, change hearing aid batteries, and handle 50-pound wheelchairs. I experienced three-doctor days—audiologist, gynecologist and eye doctor, one after the other. Now I understand how waiting rooms got their name. Woody Allen said the most important thing in life is showing up. I showed up but my learning curve was steep.

Once Dad put his mind to it, he made a remarkable recovery. He was walking and talking normally in six months. By the fall of 1996, my folks moved into the Wesleyan Retirement Home in Georgetown, two blocks from my aunt and uncle's house. This was the dreaded "home" I'd been suggesting they consider for years. Dad always grunted when I mentioned moving there, saying it was a place for "old people."

They loved it.

Dad made sure Mother got to meals on time and didn't wander. As a result, he regained a sense of purpose. Although I bought his spotless Buick, he eyed it carefully each time I came to visit. He noticed a missing hub cap before I did and resumed his long-running critique of my driving skills.

My greatest challenge was dealing with mother's memory loss. When I lived in California, I could ignore her lapses. Up close, day after day, mother's dementia was stressful. Her repeated questions tested my patience. She was no longer living in the land of logic. Mother had 60 dresses in her closet but would only wear five of them. When I asked her why, she said, "They aren't mine. They're stolen! Do you want me to go to jail?" No amount of coaxing or cogent argument could change her mind.

One day, she asked if we could visit her sister in Smithville. That would seem like a logical request, except for one fact. Her sister had been dead for eight years. I made a rookie caregiver mistake and said, "Mama, we can't go see Estelle. She's in heaven."

Suddenly Mother had to relive that death all over again. As I watched her sob, tears running down her cheeks, shoulders heaving, I knew I'd done something terribly wrong. The next day I went to see an Alzheimer's expert who gave me the best advice I ever received about caregiving. She said, "Quit trying to drag your mother into your world. She can't go there anymore. Instead, you must go into her world."

And that's what I have done. Instead of worrying about the dresses she wouldn't wear, I tried to keep the ones she would wear clean. When mother wanted to visit her long-dead sister, I said, "We'll go next week." Next week never came.

Despite Dad's devotion and my best efforts, Mother's universe slowly shrank. She asked the same questions over and over. Sentences were left half-finished. She searched for the right word and, not finding it, moved on. I learned to fill in the blanks.

Mother busied herself watering plants, both real and artificial ones. Her memory was fragile, but she still dazzled me with her wit. When told that a 92-year-old fellow resident had praised her charms, she quipped, "Honey, that's the kind I attract!"

Mom often asked if I was working because she remembered when I was an actor and frequently wasn't. She also recalled my propensity for running out of gas. For years, each time I visited her, she asked the same question: "How are you fixed for gas?" She probed relentlessly and "full tank" was the only acceptable answer. There was an upside to this prodding. I haven't run out of gas in years.

After four years in Independent Living, just as I thought I'd mastered the basics of caregiving, Mother fell in her room on Christmas Eve and broke her hip. Seven months later, on July 4th, Dad broke his. Everything changed again.

Going from independent living into even a good nursing home was a shock for us all. It was like leaving the Ritz Carlton and moving into a Motel 6. There were unpleasant sights, strange smells and discordant sounds. It took me weeks to see past the wheelchairs and hear beyond the buzzers. In time, I learned to transcend the externals. Only then could I see the caring of the staff, get to know other residents, and realize that even here, there could be laughter and love.

My view of life has changed immeasurably. I've discovered how much I have in common with the octogenarians who share my parents' lives. I found that dignity comes in many shapes, including bent, wrinkled and walker-assisted. I experienced a word that had been missing from my vocabulary: unselfishness. I learned that patience is the currency of love.

Every June, Dad and I went to the Central Texas Air show to see the B-17, his plane. He was using a walker for the first time and I doubted he could manage the half mile trek down the runway to his beloved Flying Fortress.

At the ticket booth, I had sudden inspiration. I told them that Dad had flown B-17's in 1943 when the casualty rate was 75%. The ticket-taker paused, then yelled, "Bring on the golf cart!" We wouldn't have to walk. Silently, I thanked God.

Soon the golf cart arrived. I maneuvered Dad into the back seat. I sat in the front with our driver, a young solider from Fort Hood who was wearing a crew cut and a smile.

As we drove off, an enormous lightning bolt struck nearby. In my concentration on logistics, I'd ignored the dark clouds above. I turned to our driver and urged him to speed up. I said, "We've got to get to the B-17. Dad flew 75 combat missions and he has got to see that plane!"

"Did you say 75 missions? Didn't they send those guys back after 25?"

"Yeah, but my father volunteered for another tour of duty."

The soldier turned to my dad and said, "Sir, you are my hero."

I tapped our driver on the shoulder. "Dad's stone deaf. If you want him to hear you, you're going to have to yell."

He reached to the depths of his diaphragm and bellowed, "Sir you are my hero!" Everyone in the airport heard him, even my father.

Thunder boomed as we rolled on to the runway. Lightning flashed and the first raindrop fell just as we pulled up under the right wing. The sky opened and there was a downpour of biblical proportions. All 10,000 air show attendees got soaked to the bone, but not us. As he had been 60 years earlier, my father was sheltered by the wings of a B-17.

I jumped out of the cart, and prepared Dad's folding chair as if it was a throne. He sat there serenely as wind and rain whipped around us. For a moment, I could see him as he was at 33 - lean, tanned, eyes bright, his future ahead of him.

Soon the crew heard there was a veteran in their midst and lined up to shake my father's hand. One of them asked for an autograph. Dad beamed. When the rain stopped, we sat in our folding chairs surrounded by the planes of his departed youth. Neither of us said anything. We didn't have to. Perfect moments don't require words.

Mother likes to tell people that Austin's Seton Hospital only charged her "four dollars a day" when I was born—and I'm "worth every penny of it." I spent 14 years trying to live up to her investment.

I'll admit that I didn't expect to be a nursing home regular in my fifties and early sixties. There were, however, unexpected benefits. When someone asked me how my parents were doing, I knew the answer. I could look in a mirror without flinching. As I walked into their rooms and saw their faces light up, I realized I was in exactly the right place.

Hard Won Lessons

- No matter our age or achievements, we will remain forever our parents' children. That is not an excuse for inaction.

- Never remind an Alzheimer's patient that he has asked you the same question before. Answer the third time or the thirtieth.

- When faced with a choice between your parent being right and you being kind, choose kindness every time.

- If your parent is happier not wearing a hearing aid and missing your witty repartee, that is a legitimate choice.

- Respect your parents' daily routine. It is an island of certainty in a world where they have little control.

- If you move into your parents' home to care for them and find yourself considering double murder, make other living arrangements.

- If your parents' driving becomes dangerous, take away the car keys and get them an account with Uber.

- Never say: "Things can't get any worse." Yes, they can. Your mother can break a hip on Christmas Eve.

- Remember that the quality of your parents' meals is more important to them than the quality of your conversation.

- Try not to tackle everything at once. Don't plan a garage sale while a parent is in intensive care.

- When you start to feel sorry for yourself, put things in perspective. You are not in North Korea.

◇◇◇

Jim Comer has spent more than 30 years as a professional speaker, speechwriter and speech coach with clients including five Fortune 500 CEOs. In 1996, his life took a sudden detour when both of his parents had major health crises. Jim quit his job in California and moved back to Texas to become an overnight caregiver. This life-changing choice led to 14 years of caregiving, unexpected insights, and the writing of When Roles Reverse: A Guide to Parenting Your Parents. *His book was nominated by the Writers' League of Texas as Best Non-Fiction Book of 2007. Jim's keynote speech on caregiving has taken him to twenty states and Canada. Jim worked as an actor in New York, wrote articles for the opinion pages of* The New York Times *and Washington Post, jokes for Joan Rivers, a monologue for the legendary Bob Hope and appeared on the* Today Show.

Crucial Keys to a Thriving Business Culture

Carrie Vanston

"The best companies have great cultures." "The best companies have great cultures." It's almost a mantra. Guess what? It's true. Research has consistently shown that companies with great cultures are the most likely to succeed and thrive. As a matter of fact, according to *Fortune Magazine*, its "100 Best Companies to Work For" have consistently outperformed the S&P 500 Index by a factor of 2 to 1 since 1998.

So what is a business culture? It's the beliefs and behaviors that define how people in an organization interact with each other. It's basically "That's just how we do it around here." Because we all have a million things to do, it's often easiest to just go along with that.

But the time and energy to establish and grow your culture in a conscious way provides a great payoff in how internal and external stakeholders see and respond to your organization. Having a strong cultural foundation encourages high retention, happy employees, satisfied customers, and profitability.

In addition to a great culture, we want a culture that is resilient, vibrant, and sustainable—a thriving culture. Three crucial keys to creating and growing such a culture include:

ENGAGE: Among and at all levels

INNOVATE: Commitment to foresight

TRANSFORM: Increase win-win and intuitive leadership energy

144

All three are important, but taken together they create a truly thriving culture.

ENGAGE:

Engaging is about connecting and interacting at all levels within the organization and with the organization's stakeholders. The human soul craves connection. When you're looking for ways to engage, keep in mind what we really want from our work—and our lives—is to be cared about as an individual, to have our ideas and opinions valued, and to feel we are part of something larger than ourselves.

CARING ABOUT EACH OTHER

To care about each other we have to get to know each other. Providing opportunities for employees to get together, laugh, and have fun together provides an easy way to engage and connect with each other. Celebrations are perfect for this. Celebrate your wins, big and small. Celebrate birthdays. Celebrate anniversaries. Have Easter egg hunts, festive lunches, happy hours, and fundraisers. Show people they are special and appreciated.

One leader we work with described how, after we initiated an engagement program, one of her staff came to her with a story. He had come to work the week before and was feeling down because his present project wasn't progressing as he hoped; he wasn't clicking with his team; and on top of that it was his birthday. He came back from lunch discouraged, but was greeted by streamers, balloon, a cake, and his colleagues singing Happy Birthday.

He said he knew it was kind of silly, but loved it and told his boss he would never forget it. He went on to finish the project; he's getting along better with his team; and now he's one of the biggest supporters of engagement initiatives.

When have you had your heart touched that way at work? How can you touch others?

Building traditions that everyone is involved with can be an even stronger engager. For example at TFI and Corporate Cultures That Rock, we have a tradition of designing our own holiday cards that highlight a trend or event that happened that year. Our chairman writes the verse, our creative director designs the card, and we all work together to make it work perfectly. Our customers, suppliers, and others involved with our business look forward to receiving the special cards each year and we love working together on it.

One of our holiday cards had Santa dropping off packages by drones. Another had Santa riding in a self-driving sleigh with Rudolph by his side. Our most recent theme was Work/Life Balance:

Happiness means family and friends,
And interests that give you pleasure.
Challenges to keep you sharp,
And priceless moments you can treasure.

And like at home, our work lives, too
Can encourage love and sharing.
By appreciating each one's specialness
We can give the gift of caring.

The time we spend on the cards is more than made up for by the fun we have putting them together, and by the goodwill—and business—it generates with our customers.

VALUE OUR OPINIONS AND IDEAS

We cannot live by money and promotions alone. We need more to stay engaged. Engagement comes from interesting work, and being challenged, being given responsibility. Praise and public recognition are always appreciated. Praise is always the strongest when given in front of someone whose opinion the receiver values, like a spouse, boss, or mentor.

A company can't grow unless its people grow. Learning and developing skills is another great engager. Giving opportunities for people to share what they know is a particularly strong engager. We love to communicate! How would it feel if after you attended an event, you were invited to give a short presentation to your colleagues on what you learned? Or if you were asked to write a blog or newsletter article on takeaways?

One company I work with has developers in several different places. To keep everyone engaged, once a month they meet online and save the last 15 minutes for a Culture Corner. Each month a different person presents something about culture.

Let people have choices and ask for input on what they'd like to see available for development. Surveys are great ways to find out what people want. Sometimes, I use the popular Gallup Q12 Employee Engagement Survey. Other times, I help organizations come up with their own questions.

According to Fortune, the most important element in being a "Best Place to Work" is TRUST. This makes perfect sense because if we trust each other, we can let our guard down and really tap into the best win-win solutions.

Be a Part of Something Larger Than Ourselves

Purpose is a third important element of engaging. We want to be part of something larger than ourselves. We want to more than fill our space. We want to feel our companies make a difference in the world. Organizations with strong purposes always have an advantage because people get behind an inspiring purpose and stay motivated for the long haul.

Here are the four strong purposes that John Mackie, Founder and CEO of Whole Food, and Rajendra Sisodia give in their excellent book Conscious Capitalism: Liberating the Heroic Spirit of Business.

The Good: Service to others.

This is about improving our quality of life. Better healthcare, better education, and better lifestyles.

Southwest Airlines purpose is "To democratize the skies." When Southwest came on board 30+ years ago, only 15% of Americans had ever flown. Southwest created an inexpensive, efficient, fun airline that catered to everyday people. As a result, over 85% of Americans have now flown. Southwest changed the game and their employees appreciate carrying that banner.

The True: Discovery and advancing human knowledge.

National Instruments is a great example of The True with its purpose of "Empowering the innovators of the world to do more." NI employees feel they are changing the world.

The Beautiful: Excellence and creation of beauty.

This includes museums and art galleries, but also impressing all our senses through such things as concerts.

BMW is an interesting example of the beautiful. Their purpose is "To enable people to experience the joy of driving." I recently met some BMW employees in Austin for their annual convention. They were off to the Formula 1 Racetrack to race the new BMWs on the track for themselves. Do you think they were engaged with their product?

The Heroic: Change or improve the world standing by your belief.

American Red Cross personifies this with its purpose: "Enabling Americans to perform extraordinary acts in the face of emergencies."

On a smaller scale, a fellow I was working with told me that he had been with a start-up that brought WiFi to rural communities and schools. He said at first it was so exciting to be getting customers and making money, but after a while what really got him revved up was how the schools and the people were so excited to be connected to the world.

How can you bring this kind of passion to your employees and yourself with your company purpose?

INNOVATE:

Often companies are so busy concentrating on their present products and processes that they lose sight of developments and opportunities around them for future growth. That's a good way to fall behind other, more innovative companies.

How do we avoid this trap? Regularly scan for new trends and ideas in your industry and related industries. This way your organization will adapt and takes advantage of change.

Keep a pad or your electronics near to capture ideas as they occur to you, then periodically pick and choose which ones might be worth pursuing further.

My father, Dr. John Vanston, and I wrote an entire book about finding and taking advantage of growing trends before they become generally recognized. MiniTrends: How Innovators & Entrepreneurs Discover & Profit From Business & Technology Trends" suggests finding and riding these small trends—we call them minitrends—to keep your company successful and sustainable.

Below are three ways from the book for finding and profiting from minitrends. These techniques provide foresight, as well as increase connection with your customers and other stakeholders. Connecting is always great!

FRUSTRATIONS

We all feel frustrations, those things that drive us crazy! We're stuck in the one line that's not moving. Our keys disappear just as we are running late for an appointment. Traffic is a nightmare on your commute home. It's always something. If it frustrates you, it probably frustrates others, too.

But people are always finding ways to address these frustrations. Pretty soon we'll just sit back and let our key-touch, self-driving cars fight the traffic while we order food on our mobiles while relaxing in the back seat.

Ask your employees, customers, suppliers, and other stakeholders what their frustrations are. They are often the ones closest to the action. What new or improved process or service might you offer? Your customers will appreciate you asking for their opinion.

CONVERGENCE

By combining different ideas, processes, and products, we often come up with better or new ideas.

We worked with a fellow who used to work for a large corporation where he developed smart home products. Retiring early so his elderly mother could stay at home, he found that there were few services for home health care. While advocating for solutions, he became a social media pro. The MiniTrends book inspired him to converge his smart homes, home care, and social media expertise to launch a website for baby boomers who take care of their parents~and at some point themselves.

FOLLOW THE LEADERS

A third way to find innovative ideas is to "Follow the Leaders." We are so lucky that now the expertise of so many leaders, great thinkers, and like-minded people are at the tap of our fingers on our electronic devices. Keep up with those already established in your field and similar fields to scan for ideas and stay on top of trends. Read their blogs, invite them to be LinkedIn with you, and read their Twitter feeds. Look to leaders for inspiration. Let them seed your mind for your own amazing ideas.

My own "Follow the Leader" story starts in March 2013, when an article jumped out at me, "Austin Innovator: Authors John Mackey, CEO of Whole Foods, and Rajendra Sisodia on finding the inherent good in capitalism to benefit our company and the world." The article stressed the importance of putting employees before stockholders and profit, and how companies that do this retain employees and customers at higher rates and have greater productivity, profits, and sustainability.
Fast forward three weeks and I'm in San Francisco at the Conscious Capitalism Conference. I'm so determined to go that I convince my company to pay half of the expenses and my church the other half. "Corporate Cultures That Rock" is born and I start consulting and speaking on culture, adding it to my innovating expertise. My clients say that I help them engage employees, encourage innovation, and increase productivity and sustainability.

Continuing to scan my networks for new ideas, I run across an amazing coaching program,

Institute of Excellence in Coaching. Nine months later I'm the proud recipient of an iPEC Professional Coaching Certification from one of the best programs in the country.

To this day, I follow John Mackey and pay attention to what he says and does. I also have other favorites that inspire me and I'm always keeping an eye out for others with new ideas to move me to an even higher level of energy and leadership.

What similar defining moments have you had? How can you make sure there are more of them and that you act on them?

TRANSFORM:

We've talked about engaging and innovating being important for great cultures. Finally, there is transformation. Transformation happens when we tap into our highest leadership energy, honor our authentic selves, and tap into the collective intelligence in us all.

ENERGY LEADERSHIP

We are all leaders in one way or another in our jobs and lives. By becoming more self-aware and conscious, we are better able to choose to act rather than react. When we do this, we increase our level of energy and tap into win-win energy and our own intuition. And in so doing we become better leaders and achieve our goals quicker and with less stress.

Another important element in raising our leadership energy is exploring our personal purpose and passion. Reading can be helpful here, as it reminds us of lessons learned and challenges us to think creatively and logically. Writing about our aspirations allows us to focus more deeply on our own needs. It also allows us an avenue to tie present circumstances and events to the larger narrative of our lives.

Another avenue to becoming more self-aware and conscious is one-on-one coaching. Coaching offers a focused partner for achieving your goals. Coaches help clarify goals and set steps to achieve them. They brainstorm with you and cheerlead for you, while holding you accountable. They also remind you that deep down you have the best answer for yourself.

Coaching used to be looked on as something for "problem people," but now the correlation between coaching and success has proven so strong that it's consider a "must have" for many motivated and ambitious professionals and leaders.

Authenticity

Often my clients tell me they want to feel more authentic in their jobs or lives. I tell them to ask themselves: What do I really love to do? What am I passionate about? What ways can I bring more elements of that into my job and into my life?

We, of course, want to rally around our company's purpose, but how about our own personal purposes in our life and our work? What ways are you tending to that? When do you really feel in the flow and don't want to stop? What causes it and how can you create opportunities to do more of it?

One woman I work with values social interaction, yet her job is very technical with few opportunities to interact with others. She volunteered to start a Happiness Committee and now helps set up those great events for connecting people that we talked about earlier.

If you had all the money in the world, what part of your job would make it hard to quit? How can you put more emphasis toward that part? What are your strong points? How can you use those strengths to accomplish your dreams?

A fellow I coach has a special talent for simplifying difficult business processes. He values creativity and autonomy and has a great idea for an application to support his industry. He is working toward starting his own business around his idea.

Consider your values. We all have values that can be met in different ways. Is adventure important to you? One client stepped up and started focusing on customers that lived in interesting places so she could travel more.

An executive I work with felt stuck in her job and was ready to quit. Instead she took the lead in searching for new innovations and passing ideas on to the development department. Eventually she moved to that group and feels it's where she belongs.

When exploring your passions, think about what you really love to do, what makes you unique, and how you want to change the world. Then set goals and think about how it will feel when you achieve them. Next, set up steps to get you there.

Connecting with Collective Intelligence

Finally, there is great value in tapping into our universal collective intelligence. "Masterminding" is one way to do this. Napoleon Hill's classic book Think and Grow Rich, describes how masterminding involves two or more people, coming together regularly and in doing so, tap into a higher intelligence that raises everyone's self-awareness and consciousness. These groups meet regularly to support each other's goals, share resources, share services, hold each other accountable, and just be there for each other. Amazing things happen through these collaborations.

We can become so isolated, especially if we are "solopreneurs" or lead companies with no one in a lateral position. Masterminding is a great way to support each other. Look for groups you identify with in your area or start your own!

CONCLUSION

In summary, having a great culture involves engaging with each other at all levels, looking toward the future with wonder and confidence, and looking within for our true values and passions.

So what is the PAYOFF for business? Lower turnover rates, better recruits, happier customers, and higher productivity and profit!

But the real payoff is ....

A happier, more fulfilled life for everyone.

Carrie Vanston leads Corporate Cultures That Rock which helps organizations maximize energy leadership, connection, and purpose to create better performance and profit with a strong view to the future. She is a consummate connector who enjoys bringing people together to connect, collaborate, and grow. Carrie enjoys speaking on creating and growing strong cultures that encourage engagement and innovation. She has presented at such events as Investing with Impact Conference; WorldFuture 2015; RISE; Latin America Regional Project; Women in Technology Multi-Regional Project; Laurea University of Applied Sciences, Finland; Product Camp; The University of Texas SAGE Program; World Affairs Council; West Point Society; TFI Technology Forecasting Conference; and IEEE CTCN. She is an iPEC Professional Certified Coach and an advisor for the Academy of Culture Ambassadors. She is coauthor with Dr. John Vanston of the award-winning book MINITRENDS: How Innovators & Entrepreneurs Discover & Profit From Business & Technology Trends.

You Must Be Present to Win

Paul O. Radde, Ph.D.

I'm lost. I've gone to look for myself.
If I should get back before I return, please ask me to wait.

PRESENCE: HOW COMMON IS IT?

How many people do you see on a daily basis who are truly present? Their lights are on and somebody is home? They show up, are fully there and authentic?

The first response of my audiences to that question is laughter, sometimes uproarious. People crack up. And, if they are from the same organization, they look at each other and mouth someone's name or signal a colleague about someone. Then they laugh even harder.

I just asked my last three audiences who they saw daily as present and no one came to mind.

WHAT ARE THE CLUES OR EVIDENCE?

How do you even know whether someone is present?

I think that people naturally know what presence is and when someone is present. They have their own criteria, cues and clues. One woman responded that she couldn't define it, but she knew it when she saw it. To make this very point, I have asked my companions at meetings, receptions and in restaurants, "Who is the most present of the people over there?" In seconds they respond affirmatively, usually in agreement, jointly pointing out the most likely candidate.

Observing Others' Presence Makes You More Present

Consciously observing presence in others has a useful side effect: You become more aware of your own presence in the process of observing presence in others. You tend to pay attention to how you are currently centered, grounded or living in your own body. You remind yourself through your interest and awareness of others.

You can also provide presence reminders for yourself, such as, every time you are stopped at a red light. Make this a re-entry reminder and return to being more present.

Cues and Clues to Presence

According to my field research, the most common indicator of presence, is "eye contact." If the person is really there, it shows in the eyes. Poise, and composure are indicators. Positioning of the body, such as a level head, relaxed posture, responsiveness, even agility in response are additional indicators taken individually and in combination. Steadiness, solidness without being rigid, and traction work as well.

Where do You Come From?

This is not about your ethnicity, current address or where you were born. This is about your ancestors over the centuries, your blood. Where did they come from, and what toil, challenges, sweat and sheer perseverance did it take for them to get you here?

Frequently people give thanks to those who helped them in their careers. Seldom do they acknowledge anyone beyond their grandparents' generation. Yet it is the combined effort of countless preceding generations that made this journey possible for us.

We owe them a debt of gratitude to make the best of what they have provided for us. While your survival is ensured, what more would they want for you? How would they view the current lack of presence and authenticity? And, what are you willing to do about it?

Isn't it curious that after all their effort to get us here to one of the advanced economies on earth, we lack presence? So, how can we become more reliably present when we have so little support and so few role models?

Anyone wishing to become more present, is likely to have to go it alone. You have to attain and sustain presence on your own. You cannot count on support unless you find like-minded folks for a support group. So, pay attention and trust yourself. It will take courage and perseverance.

BUILD A PRESENCE PLATFORM

Early Acceptance –> Easier Presence

Who in your family or community accepted you just for who you were as a child? This was not based on your performance, looks, or accomplishments. They just liked you for you. So, you had an early experience of acceptance from someone.

Children learn early to adapt to their circumstances of family, culture and community, even if it means creating a false self. Their aim is to survive. Only when an adult gets into his thirties might he consider discovering who he truly is. Even then, whether he chooses to "come out" as the person he truly is, a decision he has to make: whether to present as the person and presence he was created to be, a presence that is in tune with his true nature.

If you are going to seek your true self, then early acceptance without qualification or condition, helps to build a platform for your own direct and unconditional self-acceptance. The experience of having been accepted, gives you a sense memory recall of how that feels. And it constitutes an established external approval for you to be who you are.

The platform you want to build should consist of an acceptance and establishment of your core being. You want your core being to be an accurate, authentic, congruent representation of your true self. And you can build it by becoming sustainably centered, grounded and aware of what is going on within you and around you.

In order to be present, it is helpful to first accept yourself just as you are. That means finding yourself to be enough, deserving, worthy. You don't have to do anything to qualify, nor do you have sufficient excuses for not accepting yourself. You are enough already. This self-acceptance strengthens your core for supporting your presence.

Remember that you are also emerging. You will continue to deal with situations, face challenges, and make choices. You are certain to screw up occasionally. Living is learning from mistakes. That is part of being human. But you do not have to wait on some future validation in order to accept yourself. Do it right now. You're enough already. YEA!

ROLE MODELS

Who do you know or whom have you experienced that models self-acceptance? To be able to experience someone who is a living example can be very affirming and confirming. There is a degree of acceptance that emanates from a person who is present. She gives off a good vibe. In fact, you may find it a bit unusual, for most of the people you have been around - underneath it all - are not that self-accepting consciously or explicitly.

You may not know anyone who is truly self-accepting. There is little written on it, and self-acceptance does not have the popular recognition of self-esteem. But, it goes to the grain of who you are. You will be on your own some of the time. And only you can accept yourself directly and unconditionally any way.

American Idol had a 16 year old male contestant in 2017, who was simply the picture of living joy. He glowed and showed no latent fear or self-doubt. He was clear eyed with a positive demeanor. He spoke of the unconditional love and support he received from his parents. He was living proof of how well that works.

So while self-acceptance is a platform for, and essential to, sustaining presence, many will experience presence from time to time even though they are not specifically self-accepting. However, without acceptance, sustaining presence is problematic.

HISTORIC ROLE MODELS OF PRESENCE

Role models of presence can come from anywhere. Even the subjects of biographies, such as Winston Churchill count as role models for many. He not only had a sense of himself. He also was a person of substance, conviction, and his character shone through as he led England through World War II.

JFK was a charismatic individual. When I met him at a fundraising dinner, we locked eyes and I felt like I was the only one in a room filled with hundreds who had excitedly awaited his arrival. As he stood directly in front of me, shaking hands, I got the sense that he was really open and available to me.

There is the a fascination with actors, performers and elite athletes under pressure. Observers focus on their composure and presence of mind in crucial moments of challenge. There are even assessments for athletes to determine if they can "tolerate success." Some do not have the voltage to contain themselves and perform through the pressure of winning. They can't handle success.

Part of being present is occupying your body, not just putting in an appearance like the empty shell of a mannequin. What makes actors so interesting is how they manage to convincingly convey the manners and characteristics of those whom they portray. They go beyond simple modeling of facial musculature. Those who utilize "method acting," the Stanislavsky

Method, draw upon their own experience and memories to fill out their portrayal. Rather than creating an imitative mask, they seem to "step into the role," and become that personage by utilizing their distinct sense memories from within.

In most of these moments there is an internal factor that comes into play. It is difficult to validate what is going on inside that person, but you are aware of that person's inner connection, and the resulting repertoire. When Goose Gossage was striking out batters one by one, he was said to be "well within himself."

Duffers will watch an entire golf match or just turn on the final holes. One thing they are looking at is the poise of the pro. Will he keep his composure, contain himself, or choke and blow it on the final holes? What can they observe of his containment? What can they learn, adopt and use for themselves?

OBSTACLES TO BEING PRESENT

Survival is a major concern by most, even those for whom there are few realistic threats. Yet, the mentality is so pervasive that it factors into decisions and choices. If it exists in their head, it weighs on them.

The survival mentality is a major impediment to being present. The lead question one poses to oneself is, "Can I be fully who I truly am, and survive?" We typically devise a survival personage to get through childhood and into adulthood. No matter how inefficient or cumbersome the survival persona we concoct, the fact that we are still alive is "living proof" that whatever we are doing, works. We are each indisputable evidence. Furthermore, we may fear that tweaking or change of that successful strategy could be catastrophic. So, there is resistance to change and possibly becoming more in alignment with our unfamiliar, yet true self, the person we were created to be. It was our less mature choices that led to who we self-created on the basis of survival. Even so, leaving behind that proven quantity to become who we truly are is threatening.

THE QUESTION

"Can I be fully who I truly am and survive?"

Other factors constitute obstacles to being present. Due to concepts of "original sin" and the "fall in the Garden of Eden," some conclude that human nature is not trustworthy. We are full of shame, a negative emotion, taken in when we were too young to defend against it. Our body is perceived as a "haunted house" which we dare not enter much less live in. Many of us live on the porch or camp a safe distance away. We are reluctant to occupy ourselves completely.

Based on the belief that our human nature is corrupt, who blames us?

There is daily reinforcement of the distrust of human nature fueled by the media attention to criminal and terrorist acts, while billions of beneficial acts go unnoticed and unmentioned. Daily we trust hundreds of other humans with our life in life threatening situations. We take a drink of water - with possible contamination from millions of sources. Consider the chances you take driving on a two lane road, putting your life in the hands of each opposing driver, trusting they will stay in their lane.

Shame is pervasive and the most weakening of the emotions. Shame supplements and advances the concept of a fallen nature. It makes us consider ourselves worthless, undeserving. Our entire society is shame-based, making it more difficult to act outside of our survival regimens and within a mode of acceptance and self-care. Self-diminishment is epidemic.

Advertising and marketing exist to capture your attention in subtle and explicit ways. The Zeigarnik effect is a major tool in the attempt to hijack your attention. For example, who will be the Final Four for the college football playoff? If you care, if you are interested, then you have to "stay tuned." Staying tuned means that the media, the advertisers and their revenues will benefit by your tuning in to watch the events unfold on the way to the playoff game. You are captured, meeting their objective.

Social media and instant accessibility by others, leaves us without reasonable boundaries of attention or time. Being overwhelmed is common, Shortage of sleep is a major threat to health. And some vacations are now planned "off the grid" to be away from these electronic distractions.

Hollowed Out From the Beginning

The exteriorizing of the individual is cultural and starts with birth. Being placed with other squalling babies and brought back to their mother by the clock, rather than based on need, establishes a feeling of helplessness in infants from the very beginning. So their tendency is to look outside themselves for the controls of their lives. This external validation keeps us dependent on others for acceptance. No wonder being present and showing up can require so much courage to turn things around.

Review Your Experience of Being Present

What is your personal experience of being present? When do you find yourself most present? Recall the peak experiences, major memories and moments in your life. Look at a time when your awareness was critically precise and incisive. You may have had prolonged periods during which time slowed down and you were totally there, present to yourself with a 360 degree awareness of what was going on around you, as well as what was going on within you.

Time slows down with presence. Life becomes manageable. And this is different from the impatience of children waiting for their birthday when time drags on. Your slow down is due to a richness of experience. The slow passage of "presence time" is due to such a complete focus on the moment that you get a sense that time expands. Your 24 hour day balloons to a 27 hour day.

When have you been most present? And, how can you use those successes in presence to foster more times being present? What do you already know about being present?

The centrifugal forces in our lives keep us living on the outskirts of our own body-mind-spirit. Rather than expanding us, opening us up to experience, these forces have us exiled from out true selves by our own assessments of how life is meant to be and how we are to react to it.

If we are to counter these forces, we need to become aware of them, and take measures to limit their pull and role in our lives. We have to bring the centripetal forces into play.

What steps do you require to establish a practice of presence in your life?

WITHINFRASTRUCTURE™

A rash of natural disasters from earthquakes, hurricanes, and flooding has shown us what happens when a country is reduced to rubble and the infrastructure is destroyed. Once gone, it has to be rebuilt for the country to go on.

As individuals, we are not aware of what would constitute our internal infrastructure required in order to live a life inside and outside, balanced and present. We each require a greater sense of what is going on within us as well as establishing an unbreakable connection to monitor and "insperience" ourselves internally. Even a list of the full range of feelings is a start in differentiating what is going on within. What you rebuild within yourself needs to be healing, strengthening, and energizing. It has to be generative.

The following techniques and exercises will put you more in touch with your insides and internal life. Not only will they help you to become comfortable in your own skin, to be well within yourself, but also to establish a balance between when you are focused within and also able to maintain that inner focus by what you do in communication with the outside world. As you take note of what works for you, you construct your own "withinfrastructure TM" to sustain your true presence.

IMPELLING VS. COMPELLING FORCES

You want to be led by what flows through you from within, your inner sourcing, not what is "pulling your chain," and yanking you around. "Ex-is-tense TM" literally claims that what is outside of who you really are creates a context of tension. It is not representative of who you are. What you want as a centripetal counterweight is a continuing factor of "In-sistence" toward living presence.

- Follow the inflowing of your breath and the resultant boost of life within.

- Always breathe consciously, deeply, enthusiastically, and fiercely. Stay focused.

- Discover what is natural to you. Live within your own human dimension.

- Walk at your own rate and pace with traction.

- Pay attention within and around you with a 360 degree spherical awareness.

- Quiet down once a day to hear your own heartbeat.

- Meditate on your goodness.

- Develop a peaceful core.

- Live fully within your own body-mind-senses.

- Follow your heart and gut.

- "Come out" of your personal closet as who you truly are.

- Live your best, most complete life beginning right now.

If you are truly, unconditionally self-accepting and also fully present, occasionally you will reach the pinnacle of life experience, Thrival, the richest sustainable experience of your life. And you will have won your greatest gift, your self.

<hr/>

Dr. Paul O. Radde, Ph.D., provides programs that enhance professionalism through improved team relationships and organizational functioning. Dr. Radde draws on 40 years as a practicing psychologist, organizational development consultant, trainer and keynote speaker. He delivers relevant, comprehensive presentations in mindfulness, leadership, influence, positive psychology and resilience—also in Spanish. Paul authored four books: Supervising, The Supervision Transition, Thrival, *and* Seating Matters *— on management and personal growth. He has presented on four continents, to 24 federal agencies, NASA, the State Department, Wall Street Journal Sales Department, and New York City Police Chiefs. His practical and innovative perspectives develop new tools and protocols for problem solutions that achieve remarkable results. Over 5,000 participants each, have benefited from his stress management, burn out recovery, management, influencing decision makers, and meeting architecture presentations. Paul plays racquetball, skis, rides horseback and hikes. The Thrival Institute [www.Thrival.com] is headquartered in Austin, TX.*

Who's Behind the Curtain for YOU?

Nancy Hopper

The first time I stood at a microphone, I was five years old. My Dad was stationed in Taiwan and I attend a Catholic School. It was a Mother's Day program and I was asked by the Nuns to memorize a poem entitled *My Mother* by Ann Taylor. It was 24 verses long and was not to be practiced anywhere but at the school. My parents were unaware of my Mother's Day surprise. So when Mother's Day arrived, my parents were in the audience and knew I was in the program, however had no idea when I walked out on the stage and stood by myself in front of the microphone. In my strongest voice I belted out...

> "Who fed me from her gentle breast,
> "And hushed me in her arms to rest,
> "And on my cheek sweet kisses pressed?
> "MY MOTHER!"

When I finished, all of the parents were in awe and my own parents were completely flabbergasted!

Looking at one another, my Dad said, "When did Nancy memorize that poem?"

"I have no idea!" my Mother replied.

"When did she practice?"

Let's fast forward years later. I had begun my speaking career in Houston, Texas. Being a student of marketing, I ran across an ad in a magazine with a five-year-old girl in pigtails. It was a Southwestern Bell Ad. The little girl was holding a phone to her ear, saying, "Call me, I got started at an early age talking on the phone!"

I was so excited as I, too, had started early speaking on a microphone at the early age of five! I thought this would be a great way for me to use the picture of me at the microphone in promoting my business as a speaker.

My postcard would say:

"Some of us got started early. START NOW! Let Nancy Hopper set the stage for your business. Nancy has been inspiring & motivating audiences for the past 20 years. She will explode your next sales meeting or convention! Don't use dynamite, call DYNOHOP!"

Once I got the postcards back, I looked at the photo closely, again and again. This little black & white picture showed it all. There she was, the Nun. Standing behind the curtain whispering out the words to me with no-one hearing or seeing her. I had this unbelievable moment! I remembered what happened. There was the proof: her black shoe and her white habit showing under the curtain.

For years, I believed I was unstoppable and a fantastic sales person when it came to products or services to customers. When asked to do anything from the age of five, I would quickly reply, "You betcha, I can do that! Consider it DONE!"

When asked, "Can you break the existing record of our company?" "Can you lead a sales team to be #1 in the Nation in sales?" "Can you become #1 in the Nation in Sales & Recruiting?"

Nothing was impossible!

With my self-confidence I had learned to sell myself, by attracting people with my energy, passion and a belief I couldn't fail. In today's fast-paced world, one needs to have the confidence to make a lasting impression whether it's digital or face to face. Let's get laser focused and maximize your interactions in building strong relationships and have fun doing it!

Let me be the person behind the curtain for YOU!

In Front of the Curtain.

My first sales career was in Austin, Texas. I was a 26-year-old mother and needed a job. Having no degree but being a student of loving people, I embarked with a company by seeing a *60 Minutes* TV show one Sunday afternoon. The next morning I contacted the company and joined them. That was the easy part. I did not know one thing about the product except that they had a 100% return policy — life time guarantee. When I met with the owners, they asked me what my goals were and how they could help me achieve them. I asked them 3 questions:

1. What was the fastest time anyone in the company had received a car?

2. How long did it take your youngest sales person to reach the top in sales & recruiting?

3. When do I get the plan of action to get myself going?

Once I got the answers to those questions, I took off running. Literally. The only competition I had was with myself.

I quickly learned that I needed a mentor. I searched out the top produces in the company and made calls all over the nation. Once I had interviewed the top 10 in the company, I got the steps it would take for me to achieve my personal goals while helping my team reach their goals.

As a young married couple with a two-year old, money was tight. I'll never forget the day my phone bill came and when I opened it, it was UNBELIEVABLE! Making all those calls ran up a very high phone bill. Now I had to face the music and figure out how to explain this to my husband. Wouldn't you know it, he came home for lunch that same day. I quickly made him a sandwich and then nudged him with a twinkle in my eye and said, "How about a quick nap?"

When our nap was over, I rolled over and looked at him and said, "Oh, no, the phone bill came in and it is a lot higher than I expected." And he looked back at me and said with a smile, "Oh, baby, everyone has start-up costs!"

Within ten months I was at the national convention in Salt Lake City, Utah. I was being recognized for my sales & recruiting, speaking to 3000 people to share how I accomplished this achievement. (I had by then had my second baby and his shirts all said, "BURP ME!")

What was the name of the company and their sales volume when I was number one in the nation? It was a company that was 25 years old, one year younger than myself, and their company sales were 2/2 billion dollars.

The company was TUPPERWARE!

Three principles to get you to the top:

1. Position yourself with Health and Vitality.

2. Build strong relationships with customers and a sales team.

3. Keep them in Your Center of Influence.

These simple principles never get old. We just need to think about reinventing ourselves for the changes. When changing, it really just takes baby steps each day in training yourself and no one else to get it right. The struggle is real when it comes to our health, energy, breaking bad habits, listening to others who tell us we are good. It is uncomfortable at the beginning but then it becomes second nature. You have got to want to begin by looking outside of your fears and getting moving in the direction you want to go. Sometimes I think, "Why do I feel I need to do this?" Why not just live out my life with my family and grand kids?

We do not find comfort in changing. It's hard to do. But I share this because I care. And there is so much uncertainty out there, that we begin to doubt ourselves all the time. Life is for the living and we need to live it! You are never going to feel like making changes in your health unless the "wheels begin to fall off." Then we have no other options but to do what has to be done to survive. Looking at yourself and all the knowledge you have, or *think* you have, is it possible you still can be getting it wrong?

Can you be a better story teller? Do you think BIG enough to see the results you are meant to have in this journey of life?

Happiness is having vitality! I get told all the time, "I want what you have!" and I tell them, "YOU CAN!" It is going take some mind-changing and looking at who you run with for comfort. These are never easy decisions, but it is doable, and fun in the long run! Which brings me to another story:

My whole family were believers in my business. Our little girl was three years old and it was Halloween. My dad was telling her a ghost story and it went something like this (He was speaking very slowly.) He said, "There was an old haunted house on the top of a hill with a long, winding pathway. You and I walked up to the house very slowly. There were howls coming from inside the house. The door was old and slightly opened. I knocked 3 times. KNOCK! KNOCK! KNOCK! No one answered."

Then my dad asked Laura, "What do you think is behind the door?"

And she said very slowly, "TUP-PER-WARE!"

Positioning Yourself with Health and Vitality!

I have learned that either you wake up in the morning and go to work out or you are an evening person and end your day feeling great. Actually, either way works; it's the routine that you must commit to.

Having heard that some workouts are like Happy Hour, I really began to check that out. As we all know, that's not what is actually happening. The music is loud and people are young and they are moving. Well, they are younger than me for sure, however it didn't stop me from showing up, having fun and feeling great about just being there. It didn't stop me from showing up for a few years, but learned I need to shut my mouth when I am on a treadmill.

Here's another story:

I was at the Tennis & Racquet Club sitting with several women as our little ones swam in a small baby pool. My little Aaron was two years old and a little pistol. He never wanted to slow down for anything and today would be no different. At this time there were about eight little kiddos in the baby pool in knee-deep water. As I was visiting with the another mom, I glanced over to the pool and immediately noticed that there were what looked like about 20 little rabbit turds floating on top of the water. Since there were no bunnies around I knew it was my SON!

Calling his name out as fast as I could, and getting him to come look me in the eye, I firmly said, "Aaron Ace, did you do those little rabbit poopies in the baby pool?" And he looked right in my face, with a crunched up nose and raised his little pinky finger and said without blinking an eye:

"I MAY HAVE DONE ONE OF 'EM BUT I DIDN'T DO ALL OF 'EM!"

The other mom was aghast. From that day forward I never saw her again!

As we build our businesses and work with our teams of people, clients and family, not only do we want to be accountable for the good results, celebrating in our accomplishments. But more importantly we want to be accountable for our mistakes. Unlike Aaron, we must take full responsibility instead of blaming others for what might go wrong and not our way.

QUICK GUIDE on Positioning yourself with Health and Vitality:

1. Ask yourself every morning when you look in the mirror, "Who am I going to meet today to help out?"

2. Be GRATEFUL you got up that morning to go change some lives out there; people

want Vitality.

3. GET DRESSED SHARP EVERYDAY. Would *you* be attracted to you?

4. SEE THE JOURNEY WITH STORIES, and use them in your own sales path.

5. Each day make the BEST HEALTHY food choices you are able to make & DO IT AGAIN.

6. Learn to say NO to foods that BRING your ENERGY DOWN

7. SLOW YOURSELF DOWN WHEN YOU EAT.

8. RUN WITH OTHERS WHO HAVE ENERGY, AND YOUR SAME CORE BELIEF.

BUILDING STRONG RELATIONSHIPS WITH OTHERS

When you are networking or at any event, nothing is better than a firm handshake on the introduction and looking someone in the eye. Simple. Then make sure you say your name at least three times in that first meeting. Sounds egotistical to the MAX but it's not. It takes people time to memorize what your name is or much less what you do.

Try it. You meet them, then say your FULL NAME: NANCY HOPPER (Well, maybe you should say YOUR name instead of mine!)

Then with your best ENERGY AND SMILE, before you walk away from them you say their name again, and smile and say your name again.

Then before you leave that event, you make sure you say your name again, and look forward to seeing them again.

I have had people call me and leave a message that sounds like this:

"Hey Nancy this is JULIE JONES, JULIE JONES, JULIE JONES!!" Laughing themselves silly, they say, "CALL ME!"

KEEPING THEM IN YOUR CENTER OF INFLUENCE

Let's draw people, your clients in your center of influence. I am talking now about your Energy, your work ethics, your life, your FUN, what you know to be true in your business. What you know and why it works.

You know who the "good guys" are. Remember them and reach out to them often.

THE BOTTOM LINE:

People want to follow leaders who lead, have fun and know how to be successful in their own life.

◇◇◇

Keynote speaker and business mentor Nancy Hopper will help you identify your STAR clients. She is the CEO of her own company and a former radio show host in Las Vegas and is also a highly experienced health guru. She's interviewed hundreds of CEOs and celebrities, and the lessons she's learned have helped bring depth and experience to hundreds of people in the sales industry. Audiences love and relate to her real life stories. She teaches individuals and companies how to accelerate their success by building relationships, mastering resilience, followups and ultimately closing more sales. Each of Nancy's programs—with her years of experience in sales with current research, humorous stories and relatable examples—creates a learning experience that gets results and shows how to keep individuals in your CENTER OF INFLUENCE.

CardBored

Mike Robertson

It might be the most pervasive cliche of our time, right up there with "You can't judge a book by its cover" and "This is gonna be easy to fix." We've all heard it countless times and said it ourselves as though it was an original thought that just occurred to us.

"Think outside the box."

It's tossed out like a free t-shirt at a sporting event, fired into the stands at board meetings and brainstorming sessions. It's spouted by teachers, trainers and politicians.

We are constantly told that what's outside the box is innovative and fresh, and that we will find success, meaning, creative fulfillment, and the adulation of our peers when we escape our corrugated cocoon.

As Ira Gershwin put it, "It ain't necessarily so."

Boxes are useful. Gifts come in them. We save precious possessions in them. Chances are good that when you leave this world, it'll be inside a box.

But when we were children, a box didn't have any negative connotations; there was no better toy at any price than the box a new refrigerator or washer came in. That box could become anything — a spaceship, a tunnel, a castle, a race car, a fortress of solitude. Back then, we loved being inside the box.

So what changed?

Many of us lost the imagination we had as children. We lost the ability to dream and pretend and shape the world the way we wanted it to be. The box became a prison and we bought into a fantasy formula that said OUTSIDE BOX = GOOD and INSIDE BOX = BAD.

Enough. Let's rekindle our creativity and imaginations and relearn just how exciting and magical it can be *inside* the box. There are millions of people in the workplace who are disenchanted and disengaged with their jobs. And all they ever hear is that they should break out of the box.

But hold on a second. Picture yourself actually inside a big cardboard box. Look around. What do you see? Four blank walls, a blank floor, a blank ceiling. Boring, right?

The child within you knows better. That kid sees six blank canvases, ready to be covered with some amazing artwork, ready to be customized to make that box a comfortable and fulfilling place to be.

I remember when my wife and I built our first house. We moved into the new place and began to shuffle furniture around and fill cabinets and closets with stuff. After several months, we realized that there was still a cold and sterile feel, and I finally figured out why. The inside of our box was boring. We had stark white walls in every room and hadn't yet hung any pictures.

We began to paint, one room at a time, and we used deep, bold colors. In our living room, we actually painted a mural, an art deco-style cityscape, complete with a zeppelin and a movie theater and a skyscraper with our name on top of it.

And suddenly our box wasn't boring anymore. Each room had a personality, a theme, a feeling. We would spend more than twenty years in those colorful rooms.

What could you do with the six blank walls inside your box?

Most people who are unhappy at work don't believe they can just bust out of the box they're in, so they continue to plod through life, hating the fact that they're stuck. But changing jobs or burning bridges is not the only way to find success and peace of mind.

It is possible to love the box you're in. You just need to become more creative, more valuable and more enthused about your work.

That box you're in still has the potential to be a spaceship, the kind that boldly takes you where no one has ever gone before. Prepare for launch.

THE MYTH OF LIMITATION

We are fanatical about our freedom. We can do whatever we want! You only have to look at the news to see the results of people convinced they can do whatever they want.

Allow me to suggest that working within boundaries can be a very good thing. It motivates us to get creative and see how we can do great things and still color inside the lines.

One of my favorite filmmakers is David Lynch. His movies are definitely an acquired taste, often veering off into bizarre and disturbing territories which can cause nightmares or nausea to the uninitiated.

It was, therefore, an interesting situation when ABC hired David Lynch to create a network television show in 1990. How could that possibly work? How could he constrict his artistic vision and get by without the language, violence, and imagery that made most of his films such a challenging experience?

He (and cocreator Mark Frost) came up with Twin Peaks, one of the most groundbreaking, influential series ever to appear on TV. Lynch managed to walk the tightrope of TV censorship and that's-the-way-we've-always-done-it and produce what may be what he is most remembered for.

Instead of thinking of the box you're in as a prison, think of how you can work creatively within those cardboard walls. The possibilities are endless, as wide open as if I were to ask you this question: how can you fill up a box? Immediately your mind begins to consider an array of choices. You could fill it with rocks. Or feathers. You could pack it with chocolates (yay!) or batteries or books or clothes or — well, you could think of hundreds of things. So don't be limited when you consider what you could add to the inside of your box. You are more creative than you believe that you are. Let that creativity run wild and soon you'll hit upon something that could be the game-changer you need.

Contents may have settled

You've probably seen the words on a cereal box: "Contents may have settled." That's supposed to reassure us that the box had a full measure of cereal when it was packaged...but during transport, the contents may have shaken out some of the empty spaces.

If you're sitting there in your box, you may have settled, too.

Maybe your mental state is something like, "Only six years until retirement; I'm not gonna rock the boat now. It'll all be over soon."

Or you might think, "This is not what I planned or wanted...but it could be a lot worse. I'm lucky to have a job at all."

That's settling.

But the way things are is not the way things must stay forever.

I was once hired by a large church to be their graphic designer. I had owned my own graphic design business and this church had become my largest client. They did the math and decided they could justify hiring me full-time to produce their printed materials.

I could have continued to do the weekly bulletins, the quarterly magazines, the brochures, and the posters for many years. But I have always enjoyed thinking inside the box, being creative with the tools and resources I already had in hand.

I started a weekly column in the bulletin. People liked my writing and would pass their bulletins to friends and neighbors. Eventually I would publish two books which were collections of those columns.

I occasionally was asked to teach a class or speak at a retreat. I worked hard at having interesting points of view and an entertaining delivery. And one Sunday when the senior pastor was going to be gone, the administrative boss asked me to deliver a sermon.

Me! The graphic designer! This, in a church with ten other pastors, seemed like a real vote of confidence. I was asked several times after that to fill in for the pastor in front of an audience of more than a thousand people.

Finally, the church decided to ordain me as a pastor. That's not something I ever dreamed of or sought after. It was the natural outcome of finding new ways to make myself a more valuable employee, new ways to implement the gifts and talents I had.

What skills or ideas do you have for sprucing up the inside of your box? Could you be the person who remembers all the birthdays and plans parties? Could you be the one who puts together an employee newsletter? Not because it was assigned to you, but because you thought it would be a good thing to do? Are you the one who spots an inefficient system of operation and points it out to your superiors? Who finds a better source for a needed component? Who sees that moving some furniture could increase efficiency? Who discovers a vendor with lower prices and/or better service than your current providers?

If you can make one thing brighter or better inside your box, you will have increased your value to your employer. Maybe you'll be commended for it; maybe not. Either way, you will begin to see that everything can be improved. It took us a hundred years to figure out how to make a soft t-shirt!

Don't settle! Grow and expand to fill the empty spaces in your box. When you do, you'll be making yourself almost indispensable...and that's a nice place to be.

THIS SIDE UP

There's a product you can buy online that started as a joke; perhaps you've seen it. It's a blue ribbon with shiny gold letters embossed on it: "I survived another meeting that should have been an email." I fully support the sentiment expressed here. I have a low tolerance for committee meetings, board meetings, team meetings...just about any sort of meeting.

One of the reasons I get so itchy during meetings is because they so often lose their way, forgetting the main purpose or objective and instead fixating on tiny, trivial details that will have little or no influence on the success of the project.

We need the reminder that's printed on the outside of many boxes: THIS SIDE UP.

If you can keep your focus when the meeting starts to get blurry...you'll be a man, my son (apologies to Rudyard Kipling). Joking aside, every team and every meeting needs someone who doesn't lose sight of the finish line, who doesn't chase the rabbits or veer off on tangents that lead to infinity and beyond.

A major reason that we feel uncomfortable inside the box is because things are all topsy-turvy in there. The vital components are scattered or broken and no one seems to know where the instruction manual went.

Take the important step of setting the box right side up again. Perhaps things have gotten sloppy: people show up late, leave early, or use the slightest excuse to not come in to work. Maybe the machine that keep the office productive are old and not well-maintained. Perhaps management has become distant from the employees and there's no sense of purpose or teamwork.

Whatever it takes to set the box upright will pay off in a big way: increased productivity, re-kindled enthusiasm, a renewed vision that you are all moving in the same direction — forward.

OPENING THE BOX

I love getting a new iPhone or a new set of business cards from Moo.com. Besides the product I'm getting, these companies have put much time and thought into what my experience is like while I am opening the box. Every item is precisely cradled in a custom-fitted compartment in a beautiful, crisp box with neat printing on the sides. Everything fits, everything has a purpose. "Unboxing" has become a huge part of the process, and YouTube has thousands of videos showing the unboxing of a multitude of products.

How does this apply to the box you find yourself in?

In most cases, we have occasional visitors to our boxes: coworkers, bosses, vendors, friends, clients, potential clients, etc. What is their experience when they come into your world? How do they evaluate you when they see how you have customized your environment?

It's not about luxury. Or, at least, it's not only about luxury. It's really about forethought. Who's going to venture inside your box? Why will they visit? What are they seeking? What will make them feel their time was well-spent?

I have long been a fan of the Disney style of customer service. The Walt Disney Company has considered every aspect of their theme parks and tried to smooth every rough edge that a visitor might encounter. You have to wait to get on a ride? They've provided a cool place to stand and a visually-rich environment so that you won't be restless or bored as you wait. You're never far from a restroom, a trashcan, or a place to get something to drink. Your needs are anticipated and filled almost before you have a chance to express them.

It's not just about decor, either. Disney's employees—or "Cast Members"—are among the friendliest, most pleasant customer service people in the world. They will go to almost any lengths to resolve a complaint or repair a misstep.

You may not be able to build a fairytale castle for your visitors, but you can make them feel like special, honored guests when they come to your place. Offering a drink, a comfortable place to sit, a chance to unwind before business talk begins...these can be pleasing bonuses that pay big dividends.

THE BOTTOM OF THE BOX

Have you seen the TEDtalk by J.J. Abrams? You should. Abrams, the creator and director of such TV shows as *Alias* and *LOST*, and the director of blockbuster films like the most recent *Star Trek* and *Star Wars* movies, tells a great story...about a box.

He tells how he loved magic as a child and how his grandfather would bring him back magic tricks when he traveled. On one occasion, he took young J.J. to Tannen's Magic in New York, where they bought a "mystery box," a sealed cardboard box with a big question mark on the side. This box was supposedly a grab bag, a collection of magic tricks worth more than fifty dollars, a real bargain at the price of fifteen bucks.

But here's the thing.

J.J. Abrams has never opened the box. It sits, still sealed, on a shelf in his office, and he credits it with much of his success in making entertainment for the world.

Why?

Because he realized that if he opened the box, he would have a couple of new magic tricks. But if he did not open it, there could be ANYTHING inside, an infinite number of possibilities. Abrams said he realized that all his movies are boxes, filled with mystery and questions and possibility, and his creativity has grown as a result of this thinking.

That box you thought was a cage is actually filled with uncountable treasure, amazing adventures, incredible success and the secrets to a happy and fulfilling life.

Every box is filled with wonder. And a box full of wonder is a pretty good place to be inside. I can't wait to see what you discover!

<><><><><><><><><><><><><><><><><><><><><><><><><><><><><><><><><><><><><><><><><>

Mike Robertson is creativity in a loud suit. As a professional speaker, he draws on a lifetime of chasing one creative rabbit after another: music, magic, writing, acting, graphic design, painting. All those paths unite in his unique approach to speaking while incorporating innovative and surprising visuals. A nationally-known expert in designing and using innovative presentation slides, Mike was invited in February 2017 to be part of the elite C-Suite Advisors group, offering his expertise to upper-level executives in the top five percent of businesses in the USA. Mike has written four books, including The Pizza, The Peach, & The Platypus, *an accompaniment to his signature keynote speech on creativity,* The Art of Readiness. *He lives in Austin with his wife of 30 years, Lisa, a talented videographer and documentary filmmaker. They have one daughter, Lindsey, a writer and performer in Los Angeles. Mike Robertson believes that life is an art project and he tries to add an interesting page/color/melody to his own life every single day. Please visit IsThisMikeOn.com for more info.*

The National Speakers Association (NSA) is a collective of more than 3,500 members whose skills, expertise and experience power the most recognized and respected professional speakers organization in the industry.

Founded in 1973 by Cavett Robert, NSA has the comprehensive resources, cutting-edge tools, insightful education and productive events that speakers need to develop their brands and grow their businesses. NSA's members include experts in a variety of industries and disciplines, who reach audiences as speakers, trainers, educators, humorists, motivators, consultants, authors and more. There are 35 independently run state and regional chapters throughout the U.S.

The Austin chapter of NSA is home to nearly 50 speakers, trainers, consultants and communicators. We meet monthly for networking, education, inspiration, and to encourage each other in the amazing and gratifying business of speaking for a living. If you're interested in exploring the idea of speaking professionally—or if you need a great speaker for a conference, seminar or other event—visit our website at www.nsa-austin.com for all the resources you need.